MOST INFLUENTIAL
BRITONS
OF THE LAST 100 YEARS

PETER PUGH

Published in the UK in 2015 by
Icon Books Ltd, Omnibus Business Centre,
39–41 North Road, London N7 9DP
email: info@iconbooks.com
www.iconbooks.com

Sold in the UK, Europe and Asia
by Faber & Faber Ltd, Bloomsbury House,
74–77 Great Russell Street,
London WC1B 3DA or their agents

Distributed in the UK, Europe and Asia
by TBS Ltd, TBS Distribution Centre, Colchester Road,
Frating Green, Colchester CO7 7DW

Distributed in Australia and New Zealand
by Allen & Unwin Pty Ltd,
PO Box 8500, 83 Alexander Street,
Crows Nest, NSW 2065

Distributed in South Africa by
Jonathan Ball, Office B4, The District,
41 Sir Lowry Road, Woodstock 7925

Distributed in India by Penguin Books India,
7th Floor, Infinity Tower – C, DLF Cyber City,
Gurgaon 122002, Haryana

Distributed in Canada by Publishers Group Canada,
76 Stafford Street, Unit 300,
Toronto, Ontario M6J 2S1

ISBN 978-178578-034-9

Images courtesy of the Press Association, Rex/Shutterstock and Gary Cohen

Typeset and designed by Simmons Pugh

Printed and bound in the UK by Clays Ltd, St Ives plc

ABOUT THE AUTHOR

Peter Pugh is a businessperson and company historian who has written more than 50 company histories on businesses from Rolls-Royce to Iceland Frozen Foods to Stannah Lifts. He is also the author of *Introducing Thatcherism* and *Introducing Keynes* from the well-known *Introducing* series. He lives by the sea in north Norfolk, and in Cambridge.

CONTENTS

INTRODUCTION

This book, indeed this series, is the result of my reading about a book published in the USA in 1978 called *The Most Influential People Who Ever Lived*. There was no Amazon in those days so I had to ask my parents, who were about to visit my brother in the USA, to bring me back a copy. They did, I read it and was totally fascinated. The author put Mohammad at number one, though as a historian I would have chosen Jesus Christ. He did not even put Christ at number two but an Englishman, Isaac Newton.

Anyway, it inspired me and now, at last, Icon Books is publishing a series of the 50 Greatest: *50 Greatest Footballers of All Time, 50 Greatest Cricketers of All Time, 50 Greatest Rugby Union Players of All Time, 50 Greatest Train Journeys of the World* and *50 Greatest Walks of the World* have already been published and here is the *50 Most Influential Britons of the Last 100 Years*.

The last 100 years is important and I have interpreted it so that the person can have been born more than 100 years ago but his or her influence has resulted from their actions in the last 100 years. A classic example is Winston Churchill who was born in the 1870s but whose influence was in the 1930s, 1940s and 1950s. Incidentally, when I was discussing my selection at dinner parties it was amazing how many people said that they thought the most *influential* person was Churchill. Clearly, they had not thought about the meaning of *influential* rather than *greatest*.

There was a danger that I would have too many politicians and certainly there are several but I wanted to include scientists, economists, entrepreneurs, authors, actors, artists, broadcasters and others. There is even someone connected to sport in there too. Although not a player he nevertheless has had a great deal of influence on our most popular sport, professional football.

Not everyone will agree with my 50 and certainly not the order in which I have put them and there will be plenty of 'What about ...?' and 'Surely ... should be in the top ten?' If my choices spark disagreement and discussion so much the better.

Peter Pugh, December 2015

THE 50 MOST INFLUENTIAL BRITONS OF THE LAST 100 YEARS

50. SIR FREDDIE LAKER

Freddie Laker was one of the greatest, best-known and most popular British entrepreneurs of the second half of the 20th century. In simple terms, he revolutionised air travel.

He was born on 6 August 1922 in humble circumstances. His father left when he was only five and his mother worked as a cleaner. He was expelled from the Simon Langton Grammar School in Canterbury. Apparently he was constantly boasting to his friends that he was going to be a millionaire.

His entrepreneurial career began soon after the end of the Second World War, in which he had served in the Air Transport Auxiliary, when he borrowed £38,000 (about £1.3 million today) to become a war-surplus aircraft dealer. His business prospered by being heavily involved in the Berlin Airlift to overcome the Soviet blockade of Berlin in 1948 and 1949.

He sold his business in the 1950s and became Managing Director of British United Airways in 1960. In 1966 he formed Laker Airways and operated charter flights which cut prices way below the established airlines' prices.

However, it was with his 'Skytrain' flights across the Atlantic from 1977 that Laker really pioneered the cheap transatlantic flights which delighted passengers on the one hand and infuriated the established airlines on the other.

Before Skytrain it was only the rich and business travellers who could afford international flights. This state of affairs had been protected by the International Air Transport

Association (IATA), which had ruled out competition on the basis that it might prejudice passenger safety. There was therefore an inefficient monopoly offering identical services at high prices.

The first Skytrain to New York in September 1977 offered a no-frills seat (i.e. no meals) for £59 (£600 today) against the standard charge of £180 (£1,800 today). By 1980 Laker was carrying one in seven transatlantic passengers. This forced the airlines to compete, and unfortunately a combination of this with a worldwide recession and a fall in the value of the pound sterling against the dollar drove Laker Airways into receivership in 1982.

Laker Airways had carried 3 million passengers on Skytrain between 1977 and 1982 and had changed for ever the prices people were prepared to pay for transatlantic and other international flights. I remember paying £450 (£9,000 today) for return flights between Heathrow and New York in the late 1960s – and you can still pay only £450 today.

Margaret Thatcher, before she became Prime Minister in 1979, supported Laker's championing of open markets in the 1970s as he struggled with legal battles against IATA for eleven years before he was able to launch Skytrain. Furthermore, Sir Richard Branson, whose Virgin Airways owed a great deal to Laker's pioneering efforts, named one of his aircraft 'The Spirit of Sir Freddie'. Laker became Sir Freddie Laker in 1978 as well as being voted 'Man of the Year'.

Sir Richard Branson was not the only airline entrepreneur to benefit from Laker. Easyjet and Ryanair, as well as Southwest Airlines in the USA, Air Asia, West Jet and Virgin Australia, also owed their existence and success to his breakthroughs in cut-price air fares. Even so, Laker felt they could go further, and he said before he died at the age of 83 in 2006:

I think it's great they are still doing it and have produced low fare operators but if you think about this low fare operation in Europe and even the US, it's still on short haul journeys. There's no one with a dedicated low fares operation across the Atlantic.

His lasting impact and legacy was his pioneering of low-fare services and liberating air travel from the straitjacket imposed for decades by IATA in collusion with governments, many of which owned the airlines involved in a non-competition industry.

49. SIR HENRY WOOD

Sir Henry Wood is known by most in connection with the Proms, and especially the Last Night of the Proms, but his influence went much further than that.

Born in London on 3 March 1869 to a father who ran a successful model engine shop and who, alongside his wife, was a keen amateur musician, Henry Wood participated in family musical get-togethers from the age of six. At the age of only fourteen he played the organ at the Musicians' Church, St Sepulchre-without-Newgate, the largest parish church in the City of London.

His ambition was to teach singing and he composed some songs of his own but, after graduating from the Royal Academy, he became an orchestral and choral conductor, gaining experience by conducting for several opera companies. In 1893, when he was still only 24, he was asked by Robert Newman, the manager of the Queen's Hall

in London, to conduct at a series of promenade concerts ('promenade' meant concerts in London parks where the audience could listen as they walked past, the French for walk being *promener*).

Newman's aim was to educate the musical taste of the general public and Wood shared this ambition. Newman said:

> I am going to run nightly concerts and train the public by easy stages. Popular at first, gradually raising the standard until I have created a public for classical and modern music.

Newman and Wood gradually carried through their plan, cutting back on what they deemed to be trivial music and introducing Wagner, Beethoven, Schubert, Mendelssohn, Richard Strauss, Tchaikovsky, Glazunov, Massenet and Rimsky-Korsakov. Every Monday evening was devoted to Wagner and Friday to Beethoven.

Wood also raised the profile and helped improve the pay of the rank-and-file orchestral players, insisting that they stand to accept the applause alongside the conductor. He also introduced women into the Queen's Hall orchestra in 1913. By 1918 there were eighteen women in his orchestra.

Gradually the Last Night of the Proms became famous and Wood composed the work for which he is most celebrated, *Fantasia on British Sea Songs*, initially to commemorate the centenary of the Battle of Trafalgar. A highlight was the hornpipe, and Wood said:

> They stamp their feet in time to the hornpipe – that is until I whip up the orchestra to a fierce *accelerando* which leaves behind all those whose stamping technique is not of the very finest quality. I like to win by two bars, if possible, but

sometimes have to be content with a bar and a half. It is good fun and I enjoy it as much as they.

Also made famous by the Proms and sharing in their influence was Sir Edward Elgar. He was born and brought up in Broadheath near the cathedral town of Worcester, and spent much of his youth in the cathedral listening to the music of its daily services. He did not have a systematic musical education but played the organ at St George's, and indeed succeeded his father as the regular organist there. He also played the bassoon in a wind quartet and, more often, the violin. At the same time he composed.

Elgar married in 1889 and his wife, Caroline Alice, encouraged his efforts to become a composer. This led to his moving to London, where he struggled to gain recognition from other musicians, publishers and concert givers. In 1891 he returned to Malvern in the Midlands and began the composition of a number of pieces for both choir and orchestra which were produced at festivals.

Nevertheless, full recognition of his musical genius was slow in coming. For example, *The Dream of Gerontius*, performed in Birmingham in 1900, was declared in general to be a failure, in spite of praise for some of its beautiful moments. It was not until much later that the work was generally recognised as one of the great and imaginative musical creations.

In spite of this relative failure in Birmingham, one of the audience, A.J. Jaeger, was instrumental in having *Gerontius* played at the Lower Rhine Festival in Düsseldorf, where the usually critical German audience loved it. This led to a repeat performance in Birmingham and a further one at Covent Garden in 1904, and led to Elgar going to the USA where his works generally met with enthusiastic support.

It also led to Elgar producing symphonies and, at last, these were greeted with ecstasy by the general public. He is probably best known for the first of the five *Pomp and Circumstance Marches* which has become familiar to millions all over the world who watch the Last Night of the Proms. *Land of Hope and Glory* is now considered as an alternative national anthem.

Henry Wood deservedly won many honours. He was knighted in 1911, awarded the Gold Medal of the Royal Philharmonic Society in 1921 and made a Companion of Honour in 1944. In Europe he was appointed to the Order of the Crown in Belgium in 1920 and as an Officer of the Legion of Honour in France in 1926.

His biographer, Arthur Jacobs, wrote 'His tally of first performances, or first performances in Britain, was heroic: at least 717 works by 357 composers ... He remains one of the most remarkable musicians Britain has produced.'

48. SIR ALFRED HITCHCOCK

Born in August 1899 in Leytonstone, Essex, Alfred Hitchcock made Britain's greatest contribution to world cinema. He was brought up as a Roman Catholic and was educated at Salesian College and the Jesuit St Ignatius' College in Stamford Hill, London.

His obsession with crime and the police was probably caused by his father's sending him when he was only five to the local police station with a note asking the police to lock him up for five minutes for his bad behaviour. He was rejected by the army in the First World War on the grounds of his obesity.

He began work in the film industry immediately after the war and took up a full-time position at Islington Studios in 1920. By 1925 he had become a film director and, the following year, he produced his first thriller, *The Lodger: A Story of the London Fog*. It became a great success.

Over the next three years Hitchcock directed ten films, and the tenth, *Blackmail*, was converted to sound, considered by many to be the first British sound feature film. The climax took place on the dome of the British Museum and began a Hitchcock tradition of using famous landmarks as a backdrop for dramatic scenes. In the early 1930s, working for Michael Balcon at Gaumont-British Picture Corporation, Hitchcock directed the successful *The Man Who Knew Too Much* and *The 39 Steps*. The latter was voted the fourth-best British film of the 20th century by the British Film Institute in 1999.

In 1938 Hitchcock directed *The Lady Vanishes*, described by the *Guardian* as 'one of the greatest train movies from the genre's golden era' and as a contender for the 'title of the best comedy thriller ever made'. The following year Hitchcock received the New York Film Critics Circle Award for Best Director, and a *New York Times* feature writer wrote:

> Three unique and valuable institutions the British have that we in America have not. Magna Carta, the Tower Bridge and Alfred Hitchcock, the greatest director of screen melodramas in the world.

In 1939 David O. Selznick gave Hitchcock a seven-year contract and he and his family moved to Hollywood. His first film was *Rebecca*, based on the novel by Daphne du Maurier, and it won the Academy Award for Best Picture of 1940. In

1941 Hitchcock produced, as well as directed, *Suspicion*, his first film as a producer. Joan Fontaine won the Best Actress Oscar for her 'outstanding performance' in that film.

Hitchcock's peak decades were undoubtedly the 1950s and 1960s, when he made, among others: *Strangers on a Train*, *Dial M for Murder*, *Rear Window*, *To Catch a Thief*, *The Man Who Knew Too Much*, *Vertigo*, *North by Northwest*, *Psycho* and *The Birds*.

Psycho, with the violence of its shower scene and the early death of the heroine, became a hallmark of a new horror movie genre and was copied by many other producers and directors. It broke box office records all over the world and was the most profitable black-and-white sound film ever made. Hitchcock himself made $15 million from it.

He seemed incapable of slowing down, even in his sixties, and made several more films including *Torn Curtain* and *Topaz* as well as *The Birds*. He was a master of shock effects and audiences eventually learned not to be lulled into security.

Hitchcock won many awards, receiving two Golden Globes, eight Laurel Awards and five lifetime achievement awards including the first BAFTA Academy Fellowship Award. He was also nominated five times for an Academy Award for Best Director. He was knighted in 1980.

47. J. ARTHUR RANK

J. Arthur Rank was influential because he not only saved the British film industry from extinction in the 1930s but was also instrumental in building up a following for British films in the USA.

Rank was born in December 1888 into a Victorian family environment at Kingston upon Hull in England. He was educated as a boarder at The Leys School in Cambridge where he did not show any intellectual prowess.

Rank was deeply religious and, in 1933, he helped to set up a new voluntary body, the Religious Film Society. He even came up with the idea for its first 20-minute film, *The Mastership of Christ*, produced in 1934.

Rank was also a businessman and he saw films as a commodity. Like many evangelical preachers, he believed that spreading the word of God was the same as selling a product. Films, too, could be produced, marketed and sold like flour.

And very quickly the business of making films roused Rank's competitive instincts. Within barely two years, not content with funding straightforwardly religious films, he decided to make mainstream films for a wider audience, gently introducing them to 'moral' and 'wholesome' values without subjecting them to a sermon. Through films, he said, he would 'help men and women make this world a better place to live in'.

In 1935, in alliance with the Tory peer Viscount Portal, he set up the General Cinema Finance Corporation and gradually built up a film empire that would eventually include the Pinewood studios, a distribution company, a share of Universal, the Odeon cinema chain, the Gaumont cinema chain, the studios in Denham and the Lime Grove studios.

In 1938 Rank bought the Odeon Cinemas chain and in 1939 he consolidated his film production interests in Pinewood Film Studios, Denham Film Studios and the Amalgamated Studios in Elstree, although the latter were never used as film studios by Rank. In 1941, Rank absorbed

Gaumont-British, which owned 251 cinemas, and Lime Grove Studios (later owned by the BBC), and bought the Paramount Cinemas chain, so that by 1942 the Rank Organisation owned 619 cinemas. Other interests were acquired, such as the Bush Radio Company in 1949, which would be added to the interests in a few more years within this new company.

By the end of the Second World War, Rank was the most powerful man in the British film industry, although his handling of the generally sensitive film stars left something to be desired. For example, after seeing Laurence Olivier's *Hamlet* (1948), one of the most prestigious films the Rank Organisation ever made, Rank said simply to the star: 'Thank you very much, Sir Laurence.' This was not good enough for Olivier, who had been expecting a torrent of praise and never forgave him for such an outrageous slight. And the actor James Mason, who had made his name in Rank films during the Second World War, made a blistering attack on his patron after decamping to Hollywood in 1946. Rank, he said, was 'the worst thing that has happened to the British film industry'. That was clearly complete rubbish.

Rank's empire reached its zenith in 1946. By then, he employed 31,000 people, turned over £45 million a year (about £1.6 billion today) and controlled five studios, five newsreel firms, a host of production companies and almost 650 cinemas.

The late 1940s and early 1950s were the golden age of British cinema and much of that was thanks to Rank. He put up the money for classics such as David Lean's *Brief Encounter* (1945), *Great Expectations* (1946) and *Oliver Twist* (1948), and for Michael Powell and Emeric Pressburger's *The Life and Death of Colonel Blimp* (1943) and *The Red Shoes* (1948).

It was even Rank who paid for the Ealing comedies that

have become synonymous with post-war Britain. Without him there would have been no *Passport to Pimlico* (1949), no *Kind Hearts and Coronets* (1949), no *The Lavender Hill Mob* (1951) and no *The Ladykillers* (1955).

Rank himself had nothing to do with writing or making these films. His great virtue was that he gave carte blanche to more talented people.

'We can make any subject we wish', Lean said in 1947, 'with as much money as we think that subject should have spent on it. We can cast whichever actors we choose, and we have no interference with the way the film is made.'

Even Rank's great rival Alexander Korda believed that had it not been for the Yorkshireman, the British film industry would probably have been dead before the end of the Second World War. 'Any who deny what Arthur has done', Korda said, 'know nothing.'

Rank's biggest challenge was to be successful in the USA, which meant taking the fight to Hollywood or 'Fairyland', as he called it, and he saw British history as the way to do it.

He led his attack with *Henry V,* one of the most influential British pictures ever made. Not only did it boast the talents of Britain's most celebrated actor, Olivier, it also had Britain's greatest playwright. As for Olivier, he was a natural choice to star and direct since he had not only played Shakespeare's national hero at the Old Vic but had recited stirring passages on radio since the outbreak of the Second World War.

And Rank's men marketed it brilliantly in the USA. The film was shown in college towns for one night only, and in small venues, ensuring that they would be packed.

As word spread, the distributors booked bigger halls. After just twelve months, the film had already made a profit of £275,000 (£9.5 million today). It turned out to be an early and enormously accomplished example of an enduring blueprint for British success. Rank had hit on an approach that has come to define British cinema, and perhaps Britain itself, in the eyes of the world. Such films as *Chariots of Fire, Gandhi* and *A Room With a View* in the 1980s, or *The Remains of the Day, The English Patient* and *Shakespeare in Love* in the 1990s have followed the principles laid down by Rank and have proved immensely popular throughout the world.

Rank proved to be the most influential figure in British film-making and distribution, and a worthy member of *the 50 Most Influential Britons of the Last 100 Years.*

46. GEORGE ORWELL

George Orwell's real name was Eric Arthur Blair. He was born to Scottish parents in India, where his father served in the opium department of the Bengal Government. When Orwell left Eton in 1921, after a somewhat troubled childhood and failure to get into university, he joined the Imperial Police in Burma and remained there until 1926.

Orwell began to write in the 1920s, adopting the pen-name Orwell after the river in Suffolk. He moved to Paris in 1928 but after a difficult two years returned to live in Southwold, where he lived for the next five years, indulging in both writing and teaching. He also began to visit London, especially the poorer parts. He worked in a series of mundane and badly paid jobs, for example as a dishwasher and bookseller's assistant; he consequently knew the meaning of poverty and destitution and certainly wanted to promote social justice. He recorded his experiences of the 'low life' in *The Spike* and in the second half of his first book, *Down and Out in Paris and London*, published in 1933.

In 1936, he carried out the suggestion made to him that he visit northern England, by then suffering mightily in the Depression of the 1930s. He stayed in Wigan and wrote about his experiences in *The Road to Wigan Pier*, published in 1937, which describes the miseries of unemployment.

In 1937 he volunteered to join the Republican side in the Spanish Civil War and was wounded. In 1939 he was rejected for the British Army on medical grounds and became a sergeant in the Home Guard. He wrote spasmodically during the Second World War but in 1945 published his famous *Animal Farm*. It was a fierce, perhaps amusing satire on the totalitarian tyranny of the supposedly classless society of Soviet Russia.

Animal Farm was ready for publication by April 1944 but the publisher, Gollancz, refused to issue it on the grounds that it was an attack on the Soviet regime, which was then a crucial ally. T.S. Eliot at Faber and Faber also refused but finally Jonathan Cape agreed to publish it.

Orwell is best known for, and had most influence with, his book *Nineteen Eighty-Four*, which he finished in 1948 (hence '1984' for the title). It became the cult novel of the age, projecting a totalitarian future with perpetual war between the superpowers and Britain reduced to a nonentity. Orwell had a vision of Britain as 'a cold and unimportant little island where we should all have to work very hard and live mainly on herrings and potatoes'.

His books may only have been novels but their influence and importance are such that *Animal Farm* and *Nineteen Eighty-Four* are regulars in GCSE examinations.

Many of the words, phrases and expressions in *Nineteen Eighty-Four* have entered the English language, and we use them every day:

'Newspeak' – the government's language
'Big Brother' – the party leader
'The Ministry of Truth' – responsible for propaganda and disinformation
'Room 101' – the room of mental torture
'Proles' – the lower class

In 2003 *Nineteen Eighty-Four* was listed at number eight on the BBC's survey The Big Read. In 2005, *Time* magazine chose it as one of the 100 best English-language novels of the period 1923–2005. By 1989 it had been translated into no fewer than 65 languages, more than any other novel at the time.

45. SIR DAVID FROST

David Frost was the man who led the satirical attack on the complacent class structure of the UK in the early 1960s.

Born on 7 April 1939 in Tenterden, Kent, he was the son of the Reverend Wilfred John Paradine Frost, a Methodist minister of Huguenot descent. David was taught in the Bible class of the Sunday school at his father's church and began training as a Methodist local preacher. He went to two grammar schools, Gillingham in Kent and Wellingborough in Northamptonshire.

He won a place at Gonville and Caius College, Cambridge

in 1958 and became editor of both the university's student paper, *Varsity*, and the literary magazine *Granta*. More importantly, he became secretary of the Footlights Dramatic Club, which included many performers later to become very successful in the acting world, Peter Cook and John Bird, among others.

While still at Cambridge, Frost appeared on television for the first time in Anglia Television's *Town and Gown*, performing as several comic characters. He would say later, 'The first time I stepped into a television studio it felt like home. It didn't scare me. Talking to the camera seemed the most natural thing in the world.'

Frost suffered from a certain amount of class snobbery while at Cambridge. For example, it is said that the old Etonian actor Jonathan Cecil congratulated him for his 'wonderfully silly voice' without realising it was Frost's normal way of speaking. This may have sharpened Frost's desire to satirise such people.

When he graduated from Cambridge, Frost became a trainee at Associated-Rediffusion. He already had an agent, and he performed at the Blue Angel nightclub in Berkeley Square, London in the evenings. He was sharing a flat with comedian John Bird, and it was Bird who recommended him to Ned Sherrin, the writer and producer who was about to produce *That Was The Week That Was*, which was launched in 1962. Sherrin appointed Frost as the host.

That Was The Week That Was or *TW3* was hugely successful but not everyone approved of Frost. For example, Peter Cook, who saw him as a competitor, accused him of stealing material and called him 'the bubonic plagiarist'. And the new satirical magazine *Private Eye* also took the mickey.

Cook and Frost were once both at a resort where there was a swimming pool. In spite of the fact that he could not swim,

Frost jumped into the pool and Peter Cook had to dive in and save him from drowning. Cook would later say it was one of the regrets of his life.

The first series of *TW3* ended in 1963 but a second series soon began and this was followed by a series in the USA.

TW3 was followed by another satirical series, *Not So Much a Programme, More a Way of Life* which Frost co-chaired with comedian Willie Rushton and poet P.J. Kavanagh. They were soon in trouble and the series was suspended after one sketch was found to be offensive to Catholics and another to the Royal Family.

This was followed by *The Frost Report* which ran from 1966 to 1967. It introduced other ultimately famous satirical comedians: John Cleese, Ronnie Barker and Ronnie Corbett.

Frost then did a more solemn series called *The Frost Programme*, interviewing big-hitters such as Rupert Murdoch who had just bought the Sunday tabloid *The News of the World*. As ever, Frost did not show much respect and Murdoch would say to his biographer that Frost was 'an arrogant bastard, a bloody bugger'.

Frost's greatest triumph on television in the USA came in 1977 when he negotiated a deal, costing $600,000 (about $3 million today), to interview former President Richard Nixon. The interviews lasted 29 hours spread over four weeks and, in true Frost style, he managed to persuade Nixon to talk about the Watergate Scandal, which he had never done before. Nixon said: 'I let the American people down and I have to carry the burden with me for the rest of my life.'

On the political front, Frost was the only person to interview all eight of the British Prime Ministers between 1964 and 2014 and all seven US Presidents between 1969 and 2008.

44. IAN FLEMING

Ian Fleming, born in May 1908, became one of England's most successful and influential authors. Who has not heard of James Bond?

Fleming was educated at Eton, Sandhurst and the universities of Munich and Geneva but his real education came in the Second World War, when he served in Britain's Naval Intelligence Division. He was involved in planning Operation Goldeneye, a plan to maintain an intelligence framework in Spain in the event of a German takeover of the territory. His plan was to maintain communication with Gibraltar while launching sabotage operations against the Nazis.

In 1942 Fleming formed a unit of commandos known as 30 Assault Unit. It was made up of specialist intelligence troops. Their task was to operate near the front line of an advance to try to seize enemy documents from targeted headquarters. The German enemy was led by Otto Skorzeny who had undertaken similar activities in the Battle of Crete in 1941.

In March 1944 Fleming oversaw the distribution of intelligence to Royal Navy units in preparation for Operation Overlord. In December 1944 he was posted on an intelligence fact-finding trip to the Far East on behalf of the Director of Naval Intelligence.

After the Second World War, Fleming settled in Jamaica. He had fallen in love with the island when he went to an Anglo-American intelligence summit there in 1942. He had a house built in Saint Mary Parish and called it 'Goldeneye', possibly after his wartime Operation Goldeneye.

When he was demobilised in May 1945 he took up an appointment as Foreign Manager in the Kemsley newspaper group which owned *The Sunday Times*. His contract allowed him three months' holiday every winter and he took the opportunity to go to his house in Jamaica. He worked in the group until December 1959.

During his time with the Kemsley Group he began to fulfil his ambition of writing spy novels, finishing *Casino Royale* in 1952. Not everyone he gave it to was impressed. For example, his friend William Plomer said: 'As far as I can see the element of suspense is completely absent.'

Nevertheless, he sent a copy to the publisher Jonathan Cape. They too were unenthusiastic but Fleming's brother, Peter, whose books Cape published, persuaded them to take it on. It was launched on 13 April 1953 as a hardback at 10s 6d (£15.75 today). It proved to be a success and needed three print runs.

The hero was named James Bond after an American ornithologist, an expert on Caribbean birds. The fictional Bond was an officer in the Secret Intelligence Service, known as MI6. Bond was known by his code number, 007, and was a commander in the Royal Naval Reserve. Fleming said that Bond 'was a compound of all the secret agents and commando types I met during the war'.

From 1954 until his death in 1964 Fleming used his annual holiday at his house in Jamaica to write further Bond novels, and twelve were published by 1966. Reviews of the first five – *Casino Royale, Live and Let Die, Moonraker, Diamonds are Forever* and *From Russia with Love* – were generally favourable but, in 1958, Bernard Bergonzi wrote in the journal *Twentieth Century* that Fleming's work showed 'a strongly marked streak of voyeurism and sado-masochism' and the books displayed 'the total lack of any ethical frame of reference'.

Dr. No was then published and received a mass of unfavourable reviews. Paul Johnson, writing in the *New Statesman*, called it 'without doubt, the nastiest book I have ever read'. He continued: 'Mr Fleming has no literary skill, the construction of the book is chaotic, and entire incidents and situations are inserted, and then forgotten, in a haphazard manner.'

This depressed Fleming but the gloom did not last long. In 1961 sales increased dramatically, helped by an article in *Life* magazine listing *From Russia With Love* as one of President Kennedy's ten favourite books. This led to a surge in sales that made Fleming the biggest-selling crime writer in the USA.

If Fleming had received the odd piece of criticism for his books, Albert R. Broccoli and Harry Saltzman, the producers of the first James Bond film, *Dr. No*, were nervous when it opened at the Pavilion Cinema in London on 5 October 1962. The reaction of cinema distributors a few weeks earlier had not been enthusiastic and an executive at United Artists had said: 'It simply won't work in America.'

The first reviews panned the performance of Sean Connery, who played James Bond. The *Monthly Film Bulletin* called the film 'tame' and thought Connery was 'such a disappointingly wooden and boorish Bond that the film's touches of grim humour go for less than they need'.

However, the Cuban missile crisis was about to unfold and this helped the relevance of the film. By the end of the year it had become the second-highest-grossing British film of 1962. The young particularly loved the modernity of it compared with all the usual war films and drawing room comedies. And there was a beneficial effect on sales of the books. Paperback sales of *Dr. No* rose from 85,000 in 1961 to 232,000, 437,000, 530,000 and 576,000 in the next four years. James Bond had become the publishing sensation of the 1960s. In 1965, sales of Bond books were 27 million worldwide.

During Fleming's lifetime, he sold 30 million books, while 60 million were sold in the two years after his death.

The Eon Productions series of Bond films continued after Fleming's death. With two non-Eon produced films, there have been 24 Bond films in total. The series has grossed over $5 billion – over $12 billion today.

43. ENID BLYTON

The huge popularity of Enid Blyton's children's books is well known. Over 600 million copies have been sold since the 1930s and they have been translated into 90 languages. Perhaps her best-known series are *Noddy*, *The Famous Five* and *The Secret Seven*.

However, they have not been published without criticism from some quarters. Some people believed many of them to be elitist, sexist, racist and xenophobic. Some libraries and schools have even banned them and the BBC refused to broadcast them from the 1930s to the 1950s, believing them to lack literary merit.

Blyton's output was prolific – no fewer than 400 titles – and the most successful of the 'family adventure' books were the series of 21 stories about Julian, Dick, Anne, George and the dog Timmy – 'The Famous Five'. The first, *Five on a Treasure Island*, was published in 1942 and at that point Blyton planned only six books for the series. However, so enjoyable and popular were they, her readers asked for the series to be increased to twelve. Even this was not enough, and by the time 21 titles had been written and sold, sales had reached 6 million. The series was also successful overseas: Hachette published them in France and sold a million copies within two years, and they were popular in other countries, particularly Germany.

Furthermore, a stage play, *The Famous Five*, ran for two Christmas seasons – at the Princess Theatre in London in 1955–1956 and at the London Hippodrome the following year. Two books were made into films. Rank Screen Services filmed *Five on a Treasure Island* in Dorset and Rayart Pictures filmed *Five Have a Mystery to Solve*.

The Famous Five series was so popular that regular readers asked if they could form a fan club. Blyton agreed on condition that the club should serve some useful purpose and suggested it might help to raise money for a Shaftesbury Society Babies' Home in Beaconsfield, on whose local committee Blyton served. Within a few years there were 220,000 members of the fan club.

Also enormously successful were her books about Noddy in Toyland.

The first story – *Little Noddy Goes to Toyland* – was published in 1949 and sales exceeded all expectations. Children were attracted to Harmsen van der Beek's drawings and seemed to identify with Noddy who, although he meant well, always seemed to end up in trouble and looked to his friends in Toyland to rescue him.

Other Noddy books followed in quick succession and Blyton wrote a daily strip series for the *London Evening Standard* which van der Beek illustrated.

By the 1950s many manufacturers had realised the popularity of Noddy, and any department store had a

Toyland character in almost every department, whether it was toothbrushes, soap, stationery, chocolate, clothing, cutlery, pottery or furnishings.

By the end of the 1950s 20 million copies of Noddy books had been sold in England alone. Blyton was delighted when the 'little nodding man' was chosen to feature in a puppet series to be shown on ATV, one of the new commercial television channels. The *Noddy in Toyland* pantomime played to packed houses in London, throughout the UK and overseas for years after its first performance. And a film of the pantomime proved equally popular.

By the end of the 1950s 'Enid Blyton' and 'Noddy' had become household names.

Enid Blyton was the most successful children's author in Britain in the 20th century. In a 1982 survey of 10,000 eleven-year-old children Blyton was voted their most popular writer. She is the world's fourth most translated author, behind Agatha Christie, Jules Verne and William Shakespeare. From 2000 to 2010, Blyton was listed as a top ten author, selling almost 8 million copies (worth £31.2 million) in the UK alone. In 2003 *The Magic Faraway Tree* was voted 66th in the BBC's Big Read. In the 2008 Costa Book Awards, Blyton was voted Britain's best-loved author. Her books continue to be very popular among children in Commonwealth nations such as India, Pakistan, Sri Lanka, Singapore, Malta, New Zealand and Australia – and around the world. They have also seen a surge in popularity in China, where they are 'big with every generation'.

In March 2004 Chorion and the Chinese publisher Foreign Language Teaching and Research Press negotiated an agreement over the Noddy franchise, which included bringing the character to an animated series on television with an expected audience of 95 million children under the age of five. Chorion spent around £10 million digitising Noddy, and by 2012 had made television agreements with at least eleven countries worldwide.

Enid Blyton may have been controversial but she was undoubtedly influential.

42. STEPHEN HAWKING

Stephen Hawking has been both unlucky – to have contracted amyotrophic lateral sclerosis, ALS, or motor neurone disease as it is commonly known, at the age of twenty in 1962 – and lucky: he has lived for another 53 years when doctors gave him only two more years to live in 1962.

Hawking also enjoyed other pieces of good fortune. Initially he was very disappointed to learn that he would not have the well-known cosmologist Fred Hoyle as his research adviser. Hoyle had been one of the reasons Hawking had gone to Cambridge. However, the Cambridge Physics Department put him under Dennis Sciama, one of the best research advisers in relativistic cosmology and Hawking would soon be introduced to Roger Penrose, who would teach him new analytical tools in physics.

To understand Hawking's work and influence it is necessary to refer to Newton's theory concerning gravity and Albert Einstein's theory of relativity.

When Hawking gave the Waterstones Lecture, supported by *The Times* and Icon Books, publisher of *Stephen Hawking for Beginners* (now *Introducing Stephen Hawking*), *The Times* leader wrote on 23 November 1995:

PHYSICIST AS SUPERSTAR
A brief history of Stephen Hawking

When Einstein's theory of relativity was confirmed in 1919, he became a superstar overnight. Babies were named after him, so more improbably was a brand of cigar. An impresario offered him the stage of the London Palladium for a three-week run; he could name his price. Today, it may be felt, his revolutionary theories would make less of an impact on a public sated with wonders and cynical about the likely effects of new discoveries. Yet last night the Royal Albert Hall was packed for a lecture from one of Einstein's heirs, the physicist Stephen Hawking. All 5,000 tickets for the event were sold within a few days of *The Times* announcing it.

This is by no means the first time that Professor Hawking has filled a huge auditorium; he does so regularly, all over the world. His book *A Brief History of Time* has exhausted the superlatives, heading the bestseller lists for years on end. Yet his work is not exactly easy. It explores the wilder shores of science, where understanding can only be achieved by a considerable intellectual effort of the kind that modern education and the soundbite society are supposed to have made impossible. The paradox demands explanation.

One powerful reason for listening to Professor Hawking is the miracle that he can speak at all. In an earlier age he would have been long silenced by the motor neurone disease which he has suffered since he was an undergraduate, but today a computer system and a voice synthesiser enable him to write and to speak. But if he had nothing interesting to say, the fascination of an Olympian mind trapped in a broken body would long since have worn off.

That it has not is a measure of the interest people have in understanding those areas of knowledge that lie on the borders of science and theology. Professor Hawking has been criticised both by theologians and by scientists for his use of the word God: the first because they believe he does not understand it, the second because they deem it slightly improper. He is unrepentant, as last night's lecture showed. 'God still has a few tricks up his sleeve', the words with which he concluded his lecture, is the kind of pay-off line in which he rejoices.

He is led to that conclusion by an examination of whether the universe is truly deterministic as Laplace believed. At the end of the 19th century, the high-water mark of determinism, many physicists were convinced that their subject was approaching full comprehensibility, with only a few loose ends to be tied up. The 20th century has shattered those convictions. Quantum Theory, the uncertainty principle, and now the physics of black holes to which Professor Hawking has himself contributed so much, have shown us that determinism is an illusion. To hear that claim made by a physicist – of all people – is not the least of the paradoxes with which Professor Hawking delighted his audience last night.

Hawking has received many awards and honours and in 1974 he was elected a Fellow of the Royal Society (FRS). At that time, his nomination read:

Hawking has made major contributions to the field of general relativity. These derive from a deep understanding of what is relevant to physics and astronomy, and especially from a mastery of wholly new mathematical techniques. Following the pioneering work of Penrose he established, partly alone and partly in collaboration with Penrose, a series of successively stronger theorems establishing the fundamental result that all realistic cosmological models must possess singularities.

Using similar techniques, Hawking has proved the basic theorems on the laws governing black holes: that stationary solutions of Einstein's equations with smooth event horizons must necessarily be axisymmetric; and that in the evolution and interaction of black holes, the total surface area of the event horizons must increase. In collaboration with G. Ellis, Hawking is the author of an impressive and original treatise on 'Space-time in the Large'.

Other important work by Hawking relates to the interpretation of cosmological observations and to the design of gravitational wave detectors.

In April 1988, Hawking's book *A Brief History of Time* was published in the USA (it was published in the UK in June 1988). It had been many years in the making and a first draft had been completed in 1984. It was an instant and huge success and was on the *Sunday Times* bestseller list for over four years. Hawking was asked to write a sequel and in 2001 *The Universe in a Nutshell* was published. In the *Foreword* Hawking wrote,

In 1988, when 'A Brief History of Time' was first published, the ultimate Theory of Everything seemed to be just over the horizon. How has the situation changed since then? Are we any closer to our goal? As will be described in this book, we have advanced a long way since then. But it is an ongoing journey still and the end is not yet in sight. According to the old saying, it is better to travel hopefully than to arrive. Our quest for discovery fuels our creativity in all fields, not just science. If we reached the end of the line, the human spirit would shrivel and die. But I don't think we will ever stand still: we shall increase in complexity, if not in depth, and shall always be the center of an expanding horizon of possibilities.

I want to share my excitement at the discoveries that are being made and the picture of reality that is emerging. I have concentrated on areas I have worked on myself for a greater feeling of immediacy. The details of the work are very technical but I believe the broad ideas can be conveyed without a lot of mathematical baggage. I just hope I have succeeded.

Joe McEvoy who wrote *Hawking for Beginners* thought Hawking should have been awarded the Nobel Prize in Physics. This is what he wrote:

Let's review Hawking's major theoretical discoveries which might win him the Nobel Prize.

1. Using General Relativity, Hawking and Penrose showed that the classical concept of time must have begun with a singularity at the Big Bang and thus the Universe existed at one time in a hot, dense state.

2. In 1974, he discovered that black holes radiate like thermodynamic bodies (now called Hawking Radiation) and possess a temperature (proportional to their surface gravity) and an entropy (proportional to their surface area).

3. He presented a model for the early Universe called the No Boundary Proposal with Jim Hattie which predicts density variations in the early Universe due to quantum fluctuations of the vacuum.

Ironically, Hawking Radiation, his most significant work, seems an unlikely candidate for the Nobel award as it seems impossible to detect.

However, both the Big Bang singularity (hot, dense state

of the Universe) and quantum fluctuations (seeds for galaxy formation) could be proved if very accurate absolute and extremely sensitive differential measurements were made of the cosmic background radiation.

That is exactly what the COBE project did between 1989 and 1992.

Almost incredibly, since it is 53 years since he was diagnosed with supposedly terminal motor neurone disease, Hawking is still having influence. He delivered the Reith Lecture and said,

I am delighted to be the BBC's Reith lecturer and to be able to convey the thrill of science to millions of listeners around the world through my lectures. I want to encourage people to imagine and explore the possibilities of science. Both the known, and the as yet unknown.

41. BERTRAND RUSSELL

Bertrand Russell was a long-lived and complicated character but he undoubtedly had influence.

He was not only a philosopher but also a logician, mathematician, historian, author, social critic and political activist.

Born into an aristocratic family in May 1872 (his grandfather, Earl Russell, had twice been Prime Minister in Queen Victoria's reign and the Russell family had been at the top of society since Tudor times) Russell had a very unhappy and lonely childhood as both his parents died when he was very young and he was brought up by his strong-willed grandmother. He admitted that in his adolescence it was only his great interest in mathematics that prevented him from committing suicide.

He won a scholarship to read for the Mathematical Tripos at Trinity College, Cambridge and in 1910 he became a lecturer at Cambridge University. In 1912 he published *The Problems of Philosophy* and in the *Preface* wrote:

In the following pages I have confined myself in the main to those problems of philosophy in regard to which I thought it possible to say something positive and constructive, since merely negative criticism seemed out of place. For this reason, theory of knowledge occupies a larger space than metaphysics in the present volume, and some topics much discussed by philosophers are treated very briefly, if at all.

I have derived valuable assistance from unpublished writings of G. E. Moore and J. M. Keynes: from the former, as regards the relations of sense-data to physical objects, and from the latter as regards probability and induction. I have also profited greatly by the criticisms and suggestions of Professor Gilbert Murray.

There are many other quotations that express what Russell believed and which had considerable influence:

In America everybody is of the opinion that he has no social superiors, since all men are equal, but he does not admit he has no social inferiors, for, from the time of Jefferson onwards, the doctrine that all men are equal applies only upwards, not downwards.

The secret of happiness is this: let your interests be as wide as possible, and let your reactions to the things and persons that interest you be as far as possible friendly rather than hostile.

Why is propaganda so much more successful when it stirs up hatred than when it tries to stir up friendly feeling?

Love is something far more than desire for sexual intercourse; it is the principal means of escape from the loneliness which afflicts most men and women throughout the greater part of their lives.

The fact that an opinion has been widely held is no evidence whatever that it is not utterly absurd.

To fear love is to fear life, and those who fear life are already three parts dead.

The time you enjoy wasting is not wasted time.

Those who have never known the deep intimacy and intense companionship of mutual love have missed the best thing that life has to give.

The world is full of magical things patiently waiting for our wits to grow sharper.

War does not determine who is right – only who is left.

The good life is one inspired by love and guided by knowledge.

The whole problem with the world is that fanatics are always so certain of themselves, and wiser people so full of doubt.

To be without some of the things you want is an indispensable part of happiness.

The only thing that will redeem mankind is cooperation.

The trouble with the world is that the stupid are cocksure and the intelligent are full of doubt.

I believe in using words, not fists. I believe in my outrage knowing people are living in boxes on the street. I believe in honesty. I believe in a good time. I believe in good food. I believe in sex.

To teach how to live without certainty and yet without being paralysed by hesitation is perhaps the chief thing that philosophy, in our age, can do for those who study it.

Russell did not rely only on his writing to influence society but was also a prominent activist. Indeed he went to jail on a number of occasions for expressing views that were considered provocative and illegal. For example, he was imprisoned in Brixton prison for six months in 1918 for publicly lecturing against inviting the USA to enter the First World War on Britain's side. And in September 1961, when he was 89, he was jailed for seven days, again in Brixton, for taking part in an anti-nuclear demonstration.

In the 1950s and 1960s Russell involved himself in political causes such as nuclear disarmament and the Vietnam War and he was not slow to communicate with world leaders. He wrote to both US President Dwight D. Eisenhower and Soviet Premier Nikita Khrushchev urging them to get together to discuss 'the conditions of co-existence'. He received a response from Khrushchev saying he thought it a good idea, and US Secretary of State John Foster Dulles replied on behalf of Eisenhower.

He wrote again to Khrushchev during the Cuban missile crisis in 1962 and Khrushchev assured him the Soviet

Government would not be reckless. Russell sent this telegram to President Kennedy: 'Your action desperate. Threat to human survival. No conceivable justification. Civilized man condemns it. We will not have mass murder. Utilitarianism means war. End this madness.'

40. DAME CICELY SAUNDERS

What has come to be known as the Hospice Movement was initiated and led for over 40 years by Cicely Saunders. She had successively qualified as a nurse, as a Lady Almoner and as a doctor and achieved an Oxford degree in social sciences (philosophy, politics and economics). She came a long way from being an unusually tall, shy, very intelligent girl who felt like the odd one out, to joining the ranks of the truly remarkable people who have revolutionised the care of the terminally ill.

Cicely was born in 1918. At 13 she was sent to boarding school at Roedean, very cross that she had not been consulted about such an important decision. There she did all right, but was a bit lonely. A bit of an outsider at six feet tall (though she never admitted to it) and very clever she was considered rather daunting, especially by eligible young men. In 1938, she went to Oxford to read social sciences and though, when the Second World War broke out in 1939, Cicely at first continued at Oxford, she felt frustrated that she wasn't doing anything useful. Determined to go into nursing despite some family opposition, she applied to and was accepted by the Nightingale School at St Thomas's Hospital in London in 1940.

Towards the end of her nursing training in early 1944, Cicely suffered a back injury, and just as she qualified as an SRN (State Registered Nurse), she was told she couldn't go on nursing; if she did she would be in continual pain. So, very reluctantly, she abandoned her fledgling career.

She still wanted to be close to patients and she knew she could do that as a Lady Almoner, nowadays known as a medical social worker. So Cicely went back to Oxford in October 1944, to get a Diploma in public health, and to finish her PPE degree. She did all that in a year, getting a Distinction in public health. Then she rejoined St Thomas's in London for practical training as a Lady Almoner.

She soon realised that she was seeing a number of patients who were being cared for in hospitals which were designed to cure infectious disease or repair broken bones and so on, but which weren't well equipped to deal with people who were in pain and dying slowly, troubled by all sorts of non-medical worries, which the Almoners were there to help them deal with.

She became particularly attracted to one patient, David Tasma, a Polish waiter, about 40, who had escaped somehow from the Warsaw ghetto during the War, and had ended up in London. He had terminal cancer and was feeling that his life had really been worthless. He had done nothing good, nothing worthwhile. So there he was, at the end of his life. Cicely spent a lot of time with him, over a period of only about a month, and they developed a very close relationship. She recognised that the pain he was suffering had in fact multiple components, one being that he had lost his family's Jewish faith. Cicely discussed her own beliefs and life's meaning with David, and thus helped him to return to the faith of his fathers. Her observation of him and other patients showed her that if they could be helped

with spiritual issues, regardless of their faith if any, and with family problems and other worries, instead of concentrating only on their physical symptoms, then they usually settled and needed less pain control than if pain control was all that was being offered. This was the germ of the idea that terminal patients needed to be cared for in a quite different way and reinforced the concept Cicely was developing and which became known as Total Pain.

As a doctor, Cicely knew that the medical profession was very reluctant to use morphine or heroin to control pain, although they were the best drugs for it, and at the time were only given by injection – not all that pleasant for patients. Because doctors were scared of morphine addiction, they were loath to give regular amounts but waited until patients were virtually screaming for help. In her research on patients at St Joseph's Hospice, she set about determining whether orally administered morphine or heroin was successfully controlling pain with little-and-often doses, and whether there was any risk of addiction. Indeed, if somebody was dying, did it really matter?

Cicely accumulated records of over 1,000 patients while she was at St Joseph's. She took many photographs of patients, first as they arrived, anxious, in pain, generally exhausted from tough experiences in general hospitals. Photographed again after a few days when pain was controlled, how different they were – they had become themselves again. She proved her case completely. She used her photos in lectures to great effect and eventual success. She never wrote up her thesis, though she was elected FRCP because of the success of St Christopher's, the hospice she founded in 1967, and in recognition of her vast number of papers and other publications. All credit to the Royal College – her bronze bust is on prominent display there.

While she was undertaking research, Cicely began to gather together a group of like-minded professional friends – doctors, nurses and others, some of whom had been medical students with her at St Thomas's – who understood the problem. They were a vital advisory group who helped her to work out what was needed and how that need could be met on a practical level. They concluded that the answer was a dedicated hospital for the terminally ill, which should be called a hospice.

The name St Christopher's Hospice was agreed on, after the Saint who carried the Christ child across the river. St Christopher's Hospice would not only care for patients, but would also carry out research and teach other professionals – nurses, doctors and others – to use elsewhere the improvements the team at St Christopher's were making in the care of the dying. This academic approach with three components – care, research and teaching – would be a tremendous strength, distinguishing St Christopher's from existing charitable hospices for the chronically sick.

Things developed well. Cicely found she had a talent for fund-raising. She came across work by people in different parts of the world, but particularly in the United States, on the problems of death and dying, control of pain and looking after terminally ill patients. In 1963 she had been introduced to the Ella Lyman Cabot Trust of Boston, USA. They gave her a grant to travel to the United States to meet a number of people who she had already identified as being involved in this field. She went on an eight-week visit to the States. There she found that she was able to introduce colleagues in America to others they did not know who were working on the same problems.

This first visit to America, and the impact of American energy and can-do spirit, made a dramatic difference to

Cicely. She gave lectures to nursing and medical students at Yale organised by a wonderful woman, Florence Wald, then the dean of the Yale University Nursing School. After visiting St Christopher's in 1968 Florence was inspired to start planning the first modern hospice in the United States in Newhaven, Connecticut. A by-product was that Dean Florence successfully nominated Cicely for an honorary DSc at Yale for the work she had been doing in the care of the terminally ill.

By a series of accidents, some happy, others painful, Cicely followed a logical path to where she found her vocation then did what she knew she was called to do. Her vision of what was wanted gradually changed and developed to become something highly practical and effective. She had the vision, she felt a calling, she got all the right training, and did crucial research on control of pain. She also experienced painful bereavement several times, that tested but never shook her faith.

At St Christopher's Hospice, Cicely engaged Dr Robert Twycross to start serious research very early in the 1970s. Research continued there. In the 1990s Cicely saw there was so much to do that St Christopher's could not provide all the research capacity, there was a gap to fill. She knew there were major charities and donors who prefer to provide grants for research, rather than ongoing care. So in 2000, at 10 Downing Street, thanks to Sir Richard Wilson, Cabinet Secretary, she launched the Cicely Saunders Foundation. It is now named Cicely Saunders International (CSI), to carry out and promote research into hospice care.

Most of this progress is due to a remarkable series of women, some of whom preceded Cicely, and others who joined her in her work later on. They range from Dean Florence Wald of the Yale University Nursing School in

Newhaven, Connecticut, USA, and Louie, one of Cicely's favourite, very disabled and surprisingly long-lived patients at St Joseph's, to Sister Zita Marie from Kansas City, USA.

Now, fortunately, legions of such great people are working around the world.

Dame Cicely's work, and that of many others who took up her challenges, was recognised in her lifetime, with Royal honours and 22 Honorary Doctorates.

39. DAVID HOCKNEY

David Hockney is not only a painter but also a draughtsman, printmaker, stage designer and photographer.

Nevertheless his chief occupation is painting and his main subjects have been portraiture, landscape and still life. He emigrated to Beverly Hills in California in the less tolerant days of Britain in the early 1960s and found the better light of California inspiring and he produced many wonderful landscape paintings. As well as overlooking the Pacific Ocean he also attempted to portray the movement of colour in the Grand Canyon.

Hockney had been born in Bradford, Yorkshire in 1937 and after attending Bradford Grammar School and Bradford College of Art, gained a place at the Royal College of Art in 1959. In 1960 he saw a Picasso exhibition at the Tate Gallery and was much influenced by it. He was also inspired by the Cubists.

In the 1960s he soon made an impression not only in the USA but also in Britain and by the end of the decade was becoming well known in artistic circles. After leaving

the Royal College of Art with a gold medal he had his first solo exhibition in London and this was a sell-out. *The Sunday Times* was about to publish its first colour magazine and commissioned Hockney's drawings of Egypt. He won a graphic prize at the Paris Biennale and, on a visit to New York, met Andy Warhol. He said later:

> I'd spent a few months in New York. As soon as I got there I realised that this was the place for me. It was a 24-hour city in a way that London wasn't. It didn't matter where you were from. I absolutely loved it, and when I went to LA I liked that even more.

Edward White, an author, who, like Hockney, was gay, said, 'He took up gay subject matter before almost anyone else – and the amazing thing is that he got away with it.'

Hockney was quite open about his sexual orientation and explored gay love in his portraiture. He painted *We Two Boys Together Clinging* in 1961 and, in 1963, painted *Domestic Scene, Los Angeles* in which he portrayed a man in a shower with another washing his back.

He has been a prolific painter and has exhibited frequently, notably in the Whitechapel Gallery in London, which organised many shows of his work during the 1960s; in October 2006, the National Portrait Gallery in London arranged one of the largest ever displays of his work including 150 paintings, drawings and prints produced over 50 years; and in 2009, 100,000 visitors went to the David Hockney: Just Nature exhibition in Schwäbisch Hall in Germany.

Finally, from January to April 2012, the Royal Academy presented *A Bigger Picture* which included more than 150 of Hockney's works, some of which took up entire walls. This exhibition went on to the Guggenheim Museum in Bilbao,

Spain and to the Ludwig Museum in Cologne, Germany.

With all of this, Hockney's achievements and influence were internationally recognised. As early as 1967 his *Peter Getting Out of Nick's Pool* won the John Moores Painting Prize at the Walker Art Gallery in Liverpool. He was offered, but declined, a knighthood in 1990 but accepted an Order of Merit in 2012. And it was not only his painting that was recognised. In 1988 Hockney was awarded The Royal Photographic Society's Progress Medal, and in 2003 the Special 150th Anniversary Medal and Honorary Fellowship was presented to him in recognition of a sustained, significant contribution to the art of photography.

In a poll organised by The Other Art Fair in 2011, 1,000 British painters and sculptors voted Hockney Britain's most influential artist of all time.

38. DAVID OGILVY

In the world of advertising which has become such a significant influence in everyone's life today, the most influential advertising guru of the last 100 years is undoubtedly David Ogilvy.

Born to a Scottish father and an Anglo-Irish mother in 1911, he was educated at the fee-paying Fettes College in Edinburgh and Christ Church College, Oxford. His first job was as an apprentice chef in the Hotel Majestic in Paris in 1931. After a year he returned to Scotland where he sold AGA cooking stoves door-to-door. His employer was so impressed with his salesmanship he asked him to write an instruction manual. *Fortune* magazine would later describe it as the finest sales instruction manual ever written. Ogilvy's older brother showed it to his employer, the London advertising agency Mather & Crowther, who then offered David Ogilvy a job as an account executive.

In 1938 he was sent to the USA and worked for George Gallup's Audience Research Institute. He would say later that Gallup's emphasis on meticulous research was a major influence. He worked in intelligence in the USA and Canada during the War and then bought a farm in Pennsylvania. However, he did not find farming stimulating enough and moved to Manhattan, New York in 1948, where he founded his own advertising agency with backing from Mather & Crowther. His agency was called Ogilvy, Benson & Mather.

At that time national advertising in the USA was carried out not through television – only one in ten Americans owned a television set – but through radio and four major magazines: *Life, Look, The Saturday Evening Post* and *Reader's Digest*.

Gradually, the agency picked up clients and the first big one was the cosmetics queen Helena Rubinstein, whom Ogilvy would later describe as a 'fascinating witch'. Nevertheless, he charmed and flattered her and called her 'the first lady of beauty science' in his ads. Rubinstein was known for firing her advertising agencies every year but Ogilvy kept the account for fifteen years and within three weeks of his appointment a single advertisement brought in orders equal to sales estimates for the coming twelve months.

From this auspicious start Ogilvy built his agency over the following decade and was approached by the biggest advertisers in the USA. Perhaps his most famous campaign was 'The Man in the Hathaway Shirt' with the black eye patch. It was an instant success. The first insertion in *The New Yorker*, costing only $3,176, sold every Hathaway shirt in stock within a week. It was soon imitated all over the world and Ogilvy said later: 'For some reason I've never known, the eye patch made Hathaway instantly famous. Perhaps more to the point it made me instantly famous too.'

His next big success was for Schweppes and by 1953, just five years after he founded the agency, he had eighteen accounts and was ranked 58th among US advertising agencies. Another triumph was his advertising for Rolls-Royce with the headline: 'At 60 Miles an Hour the Loudest Noise in This New Rolls-Royce Comes from the Electric Clock.'

This ad, plus the Hathaway one, made it into *The 100 Greatest Advertisements 1852–1958*, a compilation of advertising classics.

In 1963 Ogilvy wrote *Confessions of an Advertising Man*, and although sales were predicted at 4,000 copies it was, in fact, reprinted six times within six months. The book was described as 'the only civilized, literate and entertaining book ever written about advertising – a magic distillation of learning and wisdom'.

In 1965 *Fortune* magazine asked, 'Is Ogilvy a Genius?' and *Time* magazine described him as 'the most sought-after wizard in the advertising industry'. Selling 1.5 million copies, it turned Ogilvy into a public as well as an advertising figure.

As Kenneth Roman, later Chairman and CEO of Ogilvy & Mather, wrote in *The King of Madison Avenue*: 'For many, Ogilvy brought salesmanship and good taste together for the first time in American advertising.'

Perhaps we should end with one of the many pieces of advice Ogilvy gave: 'In the modern world of business, it is useless to be a creative, original thinker unless you can also sell what you create.'

Here is the foreword to Ogilvy's *The Theory & Practice of Selling the Aga Cooker*, which he had written way back in 1935:

In Great Britain, there are 12 million households. One million of these own motor cars. Only ten thousand own Aga cookers. No household which can afford a motor car can afford to be without an Aga …

There are certain universal rules. Dress quietly and shave well. Do not wear a bowler hat. Go to the back door (most salesmen go to the front door, a manoeuvre always resented by maid and mistress alike) … Tell the person who opens the door frankly and briefly what you have come for; it will get her on your side. Never on any account get in on false pretences.

Study the best time of day for calling; between 12 and 2 pm you will not be welcome, whereas a call at an unorthodox time of day – after supper in the summer for instance – will often succeed … In general, study the methods of your competitors and do the exact opposite.

Find out all you can about your prospects before you call on them; their general living conditions, wealth, profession, hobbies, friends and so on. Every hour spent in this kind of research will help you and impress your prospect …

The worst fault a salesman can commit is to be a bore. Pretend to be vastly interested in any subject the prospect shows an interest in. The more she talks the better, and if you can make her laugh you are several points up …

Perhaps the most important thing of all is to avoid standardisation in your sales talk. If you find yourself one fine day saying the same things to a bishop and a trapezist, you are done for.

When the prospect tries to bring the interview to a close, go gracefully. It can only hurt you to be kicked out …

The more prospects you talk to, the more sales you expose yourself to, the more orders you will get. But never mistake quantity of calls for quality of salesmanship.

Quality of salesmanship involves energy, time and knowledge of the product.

37. ERNEST RUTHERFORD

Born in 1871 in New Zealand, Ernest Rutherford contributed to the scientific revolution that took place in many parts of the world during the first three decades of the 20th century. He won scholarships to the University of New Zealand and then to Cambridge and studied under Sir J.J. Thomson in the Cavendish Laboratory there.

A month after Rutherford's arrival in Cambridge in 1895 came news of Röntgen's discovery of X-rays. The following year, Antoine Henri Becquerel showed that uranium compounds emit radiations similar to X-rays. When he was only 26, Rutherford became a professor at McGill University, Montreal, and it was there, with Frederick Soddy, that he discovered that radioactivity is a phenomenon accompanying the spontaneous transformation of the atoms of radioactive elements into different kinds of matter. What Rutherford discovered was that matter is not indestructible. The Nature of Things, as understood since the days of Lucretius, and in some ways since the days of Aristotle, was now changed forever.

Returning to England, Rutherford became Langworthy Professor of Physics at Manchester University in 1907, three years after Chaim Weizmann had arrived in Manchester to work as a chemistry demonstrator. It was here that Rutherford was able to complete the work begun at McGill which demonstrated that helium is present in all radioactive

minerals. He identified the alpha particle as a positively charged atom of helium. By the use of a device pioneered by Professor Hans Geiger, he could count the number of alpha particles produced in the disintegration of radium. It was for this work that he received the Nobel Prize in 1908. It came as a surprise to Rutherford that he was awarded the prize for chemistry. He considered himself a physicist, and later in life he derided all scientific activity outside physics as stamp-collecting.

Something quite new about the very nature of atomic structure was on the point of being revealed to science. A discovery which would lead inexorably to the possibility, among other things, of a nuclear bomb.

Together with his team of researchers at Manchester, Rutherford conducted a series of experiments which determined what the atom looked like. It was not a solid thing, but an empty space, defined only by the movement of its outermost electrons. At its centre – and this was the revolutionary discovery – lay the atomic nucleus. When an experiment by a young researcher named Ernest Marsden established this, on Rutherford's instructions and to his satisfaction, Rutherford was to say it was 'quite the most incredible event that ever happened to me in my life'. Inside the nucleus lay almost all the mass of a whole atom, packed to an incredible density.

On his arrival at Cambridge Rutherford's talents had been quickly recognised by Professor Thomson. During his first spell at the Cavendish Laboratory, he invented a detector for electromagnetic waves, an essential feature being an ingenious magnetising coil containing tiny bundles of magnetised iron wire. He worked jointly with Thomson on the behaviour of the ions observed in gases which had been treated with X-rays, and also, in 1897, on the mobility of ions in relation to the strength of the electric field, and on related topics such as the photoelectric effect. In 1898 he reported the existence of alpha and beta rays in uranium radiation and indicated some of their properties.

After a spell in Canada, Rutherford returned to England in 1907 to become Langworthy Professor of Physics at the University of Manchester. There he continued his research on the properties of radium emanation and of the alpha rays and, in conjunction with H. Geiger, a method was devised for detecting a single alpha particle and counting the number emitted from radium. In 1910 his investigations into the scattering of alpha rays, and the nature of the inner structure of the atom which caused such scattering, led to the postulation of his concept of the 'nucleus', his greatest contribution to physics. According to him, practically the whole mass of the atom and at the same time all positive charge of the atom is concentrated in a minute space at the centre.

In 1911 the Danish physicist Niels Bohr had visited Rutherford's laboratory and convinced him that the nuclear atom explained the whole mystery of atomic structure. Electrodynamics was now explained. A nuclear hydrogen atom with one electron could destroy itself instantly by radiation emitting the electron.

From now onwards, the universe was a different place. It was not a static or solid thing, or collection of things, all indestructible, it was an infinitude of little voids, each tiny nucleus of which was potentially destructive. Mass and energy were equivalents. Matter, whose very existence idealist philosophers could still question, was charged with energy, an energy which could, with the right artificial adjustments, be tapped or controlled. Dust and stones were not lifeless. They were as energetic as tigers and much more potentially destructive.

It was a very long time before the implications of such ideas reached the public imagination, and could be adapted, with such terrifying consequences, for military or political purpose. But by the end of the First World War, scientists who had been away to fight returned to their laboratories to discover that they were in a different universe.

In 1912 Niels Bohr joined him at Manchester and he adapted Rutherford's nuclear structure to Max Planck's quantum theory and so obtained a theory of atomic structure which, with later improvements mainly as a result of Heisenberg's concepts, remains valid to this day. In 1913, together with H.G. Moseley, Rutherford used cathode rays to bombard atoms of various elements and showed that the inner structures correspond with a group of lines which characterise the elements. Each element could then be assigned an atomic number and, more important, the properties of each element could be defined by this number. In 1919, during his last year at Manchester, he discovered that the nuclei of certain light elements, such as nitrogen, could be 'disintegrated' by the impact of energetic alpha particles coming from some radioactive source, and that during this process fast protons were emitted. Blackett later proved, with the cloud chamber, that the nitrogen in this process was actually transformed into an oxygen isotope, so that Rutherford was the first to deliberately transmute one element into another. G. de Hevesy was also one of Rutherford's collaborators at Manchester.

It was also while he was at Manchester that he and Thomas Royds proved that alpha rays are helium nuclei. Rutherford performed his most famous work after he became a Nobel laureate. In 1911, although he could not prove that it was positive or negative, he theorised that atoms have their charge concentrated in a very small nucleus, and thereby pioneered the Rutherford model of the atom, through his discovery and interpretation of Rutherford scattering in his gold foil experiment. He is widely credited with first 'splitting the atom' in 1917 in a nuclear reaction between nitrogen and alpha particles, in which he also discovered (and named) the proton.

Rutherford bombarded hydrogen gas with alpha particles to knock hydrogen nuclei out of hydrogen atoms. This showed him that hydrogen nuclei were a part of nitrogen nuclei (and by inference, probably other nuclei as well). Such a construction had been suspected for many years on the basis of atomic weights which were whole numbers of that of hydrogen; see Prout's hypothesis. Hydrogen was known to be the lightest element, and its nuclei presumably the lightest nuclei. Now, because of all these considerations, Rutherford decided that a hydrogen nucleus was possibly a fundamental building block of all nuclei, and also possibly a new fundamental particle as well, since nothing was known from the nucleus that was lighter. Thus, in 1920, Rutherford postulated the hydrogen nucleus to be a new particle and dubbed it the proton.

In 1921, while working with Niels Bohr (who postulated that electrons moved in specific orbits), Rutherford theorised about the existence of neutrons (which he had christened in his 1920 Bakerian Lecture), which could somehow compensate for the repelling effect of the positive charges of protons by causing an attractive nuclear force and thus keep the nuclei from flying apart from the repulsion between protons. The only alternative to neutrons was the existence of 'nuclear electrons' which would counteract some of the proton charges in the nucleus, since by then it was known that nuclei had about twice the mass that could be accounted for if they were simply assembled from hydrogen nuclei (protons). But how these nuclear electrons could be trapped in the nucleus was a mystery.

Rutherford's theory of neutrons was proved in 1932 by his associate James Chadwick, who recognised neutrons immediately when they were produced by other scientists and later himself, in bombarding beryllium with alpha particles. In 1935, Chadwick was awarded the Nobel Prize in Physics for this discovery.

Rutherford's research, and work done under him as laboratory director, established the nuclear structure of the atom and the essential nature of radioactive decay as a nuclear process. Rutherford's team, using natural alpha particles, demonstrated *induced* nuclear transmutation, and later, using protons from an accelerator, demonstrated artificially induced nuclear reactions and transmutation. He is known as the father of nuclear physics. Rutherford died too early to see Leó Szilárd's idea of controlled nuclear chain reactions come into being. However, a speech of Rutherford's about his artificially induced transmutation in lithium, printed on 12 September 1933 in the London paper *The Times*, was reported by Szilárd to have been his inspiration for thinking of the possibility of a controlled energy-producing nuclear chain reaction. This idea occurred to Szilárd while walking in London that day.

Rutherford's speech touched on the work in 1932 of his students John Cockcroft and Ernest Walton in 'splitting' lithium into alpha particles by bombardment with protons from a particle accelerator they had constructed. Rutherford realised that the energy released from the split lithium atoms was enormous, but he also realised that the energy needed for the accelerator, and its essential inefficiency in splitting atoms in this fashion, made the project an impossibility as a practical source of energy (accelerator-induced fission of light elements remains too inefficient to be used in this way, even today). Rutherford's speech in part, read:

> We might in these processes obtain very much more energy than the proton supplied, but on the average we could not expect to obtain energy in this way. It was a very poor and inefficient way of producing energy, and anyone who looked for a source of power in the transformation of the atoms was talking moonshine. But the subject was scientifically interesting because it gave insight into the atoms.

Rutherford was awarded with countless honours during his career, including several honorary degrees and fellowships from organisations such as the Institution of Electrical Engineers. In 1914 he was knighted. In 1931, he was elevated to the peerage, and granted the title Baron Rutherford of Nelson. He was also elected President of the Institute of Physics that same year.

On 19 October 1937, Baron Rutherford died in Cambridge, England at age 66 from the complications of a strangulated hernia. The scientist, who had been nicknamed 'Crocodile' by his colleagues for always looking ahead, was buried at Westminster Abbey.

Years before he died, during the First World War, Rutherford said he hoped scientists would not learn how to extract atomic energy until 'man was living at peace with his neighbours'. The discovery of nuclear fission was, in fact, made just two years after his death, and eventually resulted in what Rutherford had feared – the use of nuclear power to build wartime weapons.

Many of Rutherford's discoveries also became the basis of the European Organization for Nuclear Research's construction of the Large Hadron Collider. The largest and highest-energy particle accelerator in the world and decades in the making, the Large Hadron Collider started smashing atomic particles in May 2010. It has since been used to answer fundamental questions about physics, by scientists who share in Rutherford's tendency towards forward-thinking and his relentless quest for proof through scientific exploration.

36. RICHARD DIMBLEBY

Richard Dimbleby gained fame and influence as the BBC's leading commentator on national, and sometimes international, events of significance. For example, he provided commentary on the following occasions:

1938 Neville Chamberlain's return from Munich after signing the Anglo-German (peace?) Agreement with Adolf Hitler

1945 The liberation of Belsen concentration camp from which he broadcast a description of conditions

1947 The marriage of Princess Elizabeth to Philip Mountbatten

1961 On *Panorama* from Berlin just before the Wall was erected, he said 'Berlin presents the most critical problem which faces mankind today'

1962 On *Panorama* at the time of the Cuban missile crisis, he described it as 'one of the most dangerous weeks in history'

1965 Winston Churchill's funeral.

Before the world of podcasts and digital broadcasts, Dimbleby dominated post-Second World War radio and television serious commentary. Even during the War he was prepared to fly 20 missions with RAF Bomber Command, including over Berlin, so that he could report to the nation the next day. He also went with the British Expeditionary Force when it advanced up the Normandy beaches in June 1944. After Germany surrendered he described the devastated interior of Hitler's Reich Chancellery.

Following the Second World War Dimbleby switched from radio to television and became the BBC's leading news commentator. People can still remember his coverage of the funeral of King George VI in February 1952, Queen Elizabeth's Coronation in June 1953, John F. Kennedy's funeral in November 1963 and Winston Churchill's funeral in January 1965.

He took part in the first Eurovision television relay in 1951 as well as the first live television broadcast from the Soviet Union in 1961. As well as these serious occasions, Dimbleby was also involved in less serious programmes, hosting the *Down Your Way* series and being a panel member on *Twenty Questions*. Back on the serious front, from 1955 he hosted the current affairs series *Panorama*. Not only was he the anchorman, he also conducted many of the interviews.

Regrettably, Dimbleby was diagnosed with cancer and died at the young age of 52 in 1965. St Thomas's Hospital announced his death just after 9pm and, at 10pm, Frank Gillard, the Director of Radio Broadcasting, announced on BBC television and radio:

This is news that will bring sorrow to almost every home in England, and the sense of deep personal loss to millions of people, in Britain and the world, who never had the chance of meeting him but who nevertheless have long regarded Richard Dimbleby as a close family friend.

Huw Wheldon, the Controller of Television Programmes, added:

> He was the voice of the BBC on thousands of occasions, and on hundreds of occasions I think he was even the voice of the nation. To an extent, I think, incomparable in the history of radio and television so far as this country is concerned, he was the voice of our generation, and probably the most telling voice on BBC radio or television of any kind in this country so far. It is in this sense I feel he is irreplaceable, and what can we do except mourn him?

Letters poured in and this was typical of what they said: 'As a nation we have lost the greatest ever broadcaster, and television for me is now dimmed and quite desolate.'

On 4 January 1966 a Memorial Service was held in Westminster Abbey which was watched live by 5 million people on television and listened to as a recording by 6.5 million people later that night. An admirer said: 'If Reith created the BBC, Richard Dimbleby was its voice'.

35. RICHARD CURTIS

Richard Curtis, born in 1956, has become one of Britain's most successful – and influential – screenwriters, producers and film directors.

His best-known romantic and comedy films are *Four Weddings and a Funeral*, *Bridget Jones's Diary*, *Notting Hill* and *Love Actually* and he is also famous for the sitcoms *Blackadder*, *Mr Bean* and *The Vicar of Dibley*.

Educated at Papplewick School in Ascot and Appleton Grammar School in Warrington he won a scholarship to the famous public school, Harrow where, as head boy, he abolished fagging. He went on to Christ Church College at Oxford where he achieved a first class degree in English Language and Literature. It was at Oxford that he met Rowan Atkinson and they both became part of the script writing team of the Etceteras revue at the Experimental Theatre Club. Curtis and Atkinson performed for the Oxford Revue at the Edinburgh Fringe show. Thanks to their performance they were invited to write *The Atkinson People* for BBC Radio 3 in 1978.

This led to Curtis writing comedy for both films and television and he wrote regularly for the TV series *Not the Nine O'Clock News*. He became nationally famous for his writing, first with the help of Rowan Atkinson, and then with Ben Elton, of the *Blackadder* series which was broadcast initially from 1983 to 1989 and which covered historical periods in British history from Norman times to the First World War. It was a huge achievement to win national, even international, acclaim for a series that made fun of trench life in the First World War.

This series was followed by the comedy series starring Rowan Atkinson, *Mr Bean*, which was broadcast in the first half of the 1990s. At the same time, Curtis began writing scripts for feature films beginning with *The Tall Guy* in 1989. As well as Rowan Atkinson, Emma Thompson starred in this film. In 1994 he wrote the comedy series in which Dawn French starred, *The Vicar of Dibley*.

His first big film success was *Four Weddings and a Funeral* starring Hugh Grant. Although produced on a limited budget by Working Title Films, it became Britain's top-grossing film at that time. Curtis received an Oscar nomination for his script and the film was also nominated in the Best Picture

category. His next film, *Notting Hill*, again starring Hugh Grant, replaced *Four Weddings* as Britain's top-grossing film. This was followed by *Bridget Jones's Diary* which he adapted from a novel by Helen Fielding.

Then came the hugely successful *Love Actually* which featured a range of Britain's best-loved stars including Hugh Grant, Colin Firth, Bill Nighy, Emma Thompson, Liam Neeson, Alan Rickman and Keira Knightley. It became a Christmas staple broadcast every year. The *Guardian* compared a speech by the Prime Minister, David Cameron, unfavourably with a speech by Prime Minister Hugh Grant in *Love Actually*.

His next film, *The Girl in the Café*, won three Emmy Awards in 2006 including the Prime Time Emmy Award for Outstanding Writing presented to Curtis himself. In 2007 he received the BAFTA Fellowship at the British Academy Television Awards for his successful career in film and television and for his charity work.

On the charity front Curtis co-founded and co-created *Comic Relief* and *Red Nose Day* in conjunction with Lenny Henry. He is also the founder of *Make Poverty History*, and, with Bob Geldof, he organised the Live 8 concerts to publicise poverty, particularly in Africa.

34. MARY QUANT

This is what Mary Quant wrote about the fashion world as she found it in the 1950s: 'Fashion in the early half of the twentieth century was the preserve of the grand, not something for ordinary everyday women. It was not seen as a very English thing to do, much the same as going abroad. Before the war it was only the rich and a few academics who left British shores. Upper-class young men were encouraged to travel through Europe, especially Italy, before they thought about marriage. Wild oats were sown and sophistication achieved this way, after a rather wild and indulgent time at university. Girls only went abroad to finishing schools to polish them for a better marriage. In the early fifties you were only allowed to take £25 in foreign currency out of the country each year, and many people did not realise that they could actually go to France with only this amount of money.

As far as fashion was concerned, middle- and upper-class men had tailors, but women's fashion was thought a frivolous extravagance. Quite grand young women had to have their frocks made by aged retainers retired off in the upstairs attics of Victorian-style households. Young women would point out the charms of some delicious dress in French *Vogue* and Mabel the ex-nanny would have a bash at making it, with some heavy fabric bought, reduced, in Jacqmar's sale. The poor girls then had to compete with a chic debutante over from Paris. No wonder our fashion reputation was a joke. In Alexander's [McQueen] mother's family it was thought laughably extravagant that one of the wives went to London once a week to have her hair done. After all, the cook could have done it for nothing – and washed it in Lifebuoy carbolic soap, no doubt.

So Englishwomen always looked best in the country, where masculine tweeds, Hunter boots and fishing hats, or jodhpurs and riding jackets, are so attractive – but they looked a disaster once they dressed up for a special occasion, a ball or a wedding. Englishmen didn't generally mind this as they usually expected to marry a woman and

leave her in the country during the week while they visited their London club – and studied the London talent, of course. The wife's hats would come out of the attic and be rehashed for all occasions. Enough clothes for several generations would be found there. Englishmen also often inherited their clothes, but at least they were carefully altered by terrific London tailors. New things were not much admired – it was seen as déclassé, like having to buy your own furniture.

After the war, Nancy Mitford must have been one of the first Englishwomen to have the guts to buy a Paris couture dress – Dior, my God. And buy it herself for good measure. Nancy was an emancipated woman but it shocked her family. So it's not surprising that Englishwomen were generally regarded as being good looking but without style.

No wonder many British women joined the Wrens, to wear a terrifically chic uniform.

What I loathed was the unsexiness, the lack of gaiety, the formal stuffiness of the look that was said to be fashion. I wanted clothes that were much more for life – much more for real people, much more for being young and alive in.'

She was determined to try something new, more stylish and more adventurous. In 1955, fashion was not designed for young people. In that year she opened Bazaar on the King's Road in Chelsea and created eye-catching displays in the window to attract customers. Her clothes had simple designs but strong colours such as scarlet, prune and green. Furthermore, her prices were keen. Her Bazaar became known as 'the grandmother of all little shops'.

Quant said, 'I want relaxed clothes, suited to the actions of normal life.'

Needless to say, others, seeing Quant's success, copied her. For example, Vanessa Denza, the 22-year-old buyer at

21 Shop, an in-store boutique set up by the traditional store Woollards, in 1961, worked closely with design talent at the Royal College of Art and could organise the design and production of 1,000 dresses in a week and sell them all within a week. Other retailers, such as Young Jaeger, Harrods' Way In and Miss Selfridge soon followed.

As Quant said later, 'Snobbery has gone out of fashion, and in our shops you will find duchesses jostling with typists to buy the same dresses.'

She was successful enough to be able to open a second branch in Knightsbridge in 1963 and she launched the Ginger Group, a low-priced line to appeal to more potential customers.

She is perhaps most famous for her mini-skirts. She did not invent the mini-skirt but she was undoubtedly responsible for popularising it.

Quant would say later:

It was the girls on the King's Road who invented the mini. I was making easy, youthful, simple clothes, in which you could move, in which you could run and jump, and we would make the length the customer wanted. I wore them very short and the customers would say, 'shorter, shorter'.

Quant certainly gave the mini-skirt its name, naming it after her favourite car, the Mini, and said of its wearers, 'They are curiously feminine, but their femininity lies in their attitude rather than in their appearance ... She enjoys being noticed, but wittily. She is lively, positive and opinionated.'

In the early 1960s she made the breakthrough when her designs were bought by the American chain store JCPenney, and the Quant label spread throughout the world of accessories and make-up.

Quant fitted into the 'Swinging Sixties' perfectly. London was now being seen as a city in which talented young people, whatever their background, could succeed and Quant showed that women, not just men, could be professionally successful.

And the new fashions of London spread across the world. Paris, the traditional centre of clothing design, had focussed on made-to-measure garments for the wealthy and elite. Now it had to reach out to younger, less well-off women and ready-to-wear boutiques with concessions in department stores opened. The USA also imported London designs and boutiques flourished in many of the major cities, especially New York.

33. ALAN TURING

Alan Turing is generally considered to be the founder of computer science in Britain as well as of artificial intelligence. His father, Julius Turing, worked in the Indian Civil Service but Turing was born in Paddington, London on 23 June 1912 because his father and mother, Ethel (daughter of Edward Stoney, chief engineer of the Madras Railways), wanted to bring up their children in England. Nevertheless, Julius remained active in the Indian Civil Service and consequently, Alan and his brother spent long periods with a retired Army couple in St Leonards on Sea near Hastings in Sussex.

The headmistress at the day school in St Leonards on Sea soon recognised Turing's intellectual prowess when he went there at the age of six. However, when, in 1926 at the age of thirteen, Turing went on to the well-known public school Sherborne, in Dorset, his preference for mathematics and science did not bring unanimous approval and the headmaster wrote to his parents, 'I hope he will not fall between two stools. If he is to stay at public school, he must aim at becoming *educated*. If he is to be solely a *Scientific Specialist*, he his wasting his time at a public school.'

In 1931 Turing went up to King's College, Cambridge and graduated with a First-Class Honours degree in 1934. In the second half of the 1930s Turing developed a computer which became known as the Turing machine. It proved that such a machine would be capable of performing any conceivable mathematical computation if it were presented as an algorithm. Turing's machines are still a central object of study in the theory of computation.

In 1936 Turing went to Princeton University where he continued with his study of mathematics and also cryptology. He also built three or four stages of an electro-mechanical binary multiplier.

In 1938 Turing returned to the UK and worked part-time with the Government Code and Cypher School (GC&CS). In the Second World War he became a leading participant in the breaking of German ciphers at Bletchley Park. The well-known historian Asa Briggs who also worked at Bletchley Park said, 'You needed exceptional talent, you needed genius at Bletchley and Turing's was that genius.'

During the War Turing made five major cryptanalytical advances:

He specified the *bombe* – the decrypting of Enigma code messages
He deduced the indicator procedure used by the German navy
He developed a statistical procedure for making more efficient use of the bombes dubbed *Banburismus*

He developed a procedure for working out the cam settings of the wheels of the Lorenz SZ 40/42 dubbed *Turingery*

Finally, he developed a portable secure voice scrambler at Hanslope Park which was codenamed *Delilah*.

Put simply, Turing's *bombe* meant that messages sent by the Luftwaffe could be decoded, allowing the RAF to overcome their German counterparts so that Hitler's invasion of Britain had to be postponed and finally abandoned. Prime Minister Winston Churchill went to Bletchley Park to meet Turing and his fellow code breakers describing them as 'the geese that lay the golden eggs – and never cackle'.

When the team at Bletchley Park found themselves overwhelmed by intercepted German messages, Turing and others wrote to Churchill:

Dear Prime Minister,

Some weeks ago you paid us the honour of a visit, and we believe that you regard our work as important. You will have seen that we have been well supplied with the 'bombes' for the breaking of the German Enigma codes. We think, however, that you ought to know that this work is being held up, and in some cases is not being done at all, principally because we cannot get sufficient staff to deal with it ... we despair of any early improvement without your intervention.

Churchill responded:

Action this Day
Make sure that they have all that they want on extreme priority and report to me that this has been done.

Churchill wrote later, 'The only thing that ever frightened me during the war was the U-Boat peril.' This was one of the dangers that the team at Bletchley were working on.

As Nigel Cawthorne wrote in *The Enigma Man,*

> With the wolf packs defeated in the North Atlantic and the United States joining the war on the Allies' side … not only was Britain saved from starvation, but it was possible to stockpile men and munitions in the British Isles ready for the invasion of Normandy in 1944. And the man responsible for that was Alan Turing.

After the War, Turing lived in London and worked on the design of the ACE (Automatic Computing Engine) at the National Physical Laboratory. Many computers around the world owe much to this work.

In 1948 Turing was appointed Reader in the Mathematics Department of the University of Manchester and in 1949 he became Deputy Director of the Computing Laboratory working on software for the earliest stored-programme computers. At this time he also invented the 'LU (Lower Upper) decomposition method' which is still used for solving matrix equations.

Turing died in 1954. It was assumed he had committed suicide following his conviction for gross indecency due to his homosexual activity, though doubts have been raised about this. In the years since and increasingly, as time goes by, there have been tributes to his beneficial influence, and in 2013 an official public apology was made to his family on behalf of the British Government.

In 1999 *Time* magazine named him as one of the 100 Most Important People of the 20th Century and wrote, 'The fact remains that everyone who taps at a keyboard, opening a spreadsheet or a word-processing program, is working on an incarnation of a Turing machine.'

In 2002 Turing was ranked 21st in the BBC poll of the 100 Greatest Britons.

32. SIR JOHN REITH

John, later Baron, Reith, born in 1889, became the first General Manager at the British Broadcasting Company (BBC) when it was founded in 1922. In 1923 he became Managing Director and, in 1927, Director-General.

Reith had had no broadcasting experience when he applied for the job of general manager. After service in the First World War he had returned to Glasgow (he had been educated at The Glasgow Academy before going to the private school Gresham's, in Norfolk) to become general manager of an engineering firm. In 1922 he went to London as secretary to the London Conservative group of MPs in the General Election that year.

He said himself that he was 'confronted with problems of which I had no experience; copyright and performing rights; Marconi patents; associations of concert artists, authors, playwrights, composers, music publishers, theatre managers, wireless manufacturers.' Reith wrote in his diary that he was 'properly grateful to God' for arranging his appointment.

He moved fast. At the BBC offices at Savoy Hill he increased the staff from 4 to 350 in a year, ordering them to work twelve hours a day as he did. He organised the broadcasting of King George V's opening speech at the Wembley British Empire Exhibition in 1924. Ten million people listened to it.

Reith was destined to be involved in many disputes and controversies and the first one of significance occurred in 1926 when he came into conflict with the Government over the General Strike. Initially the BBC reported all sides in the dispute including the views of the TUC but when Reith attempted to arrange a broadcast by the opposition Labour Party it was vetoed by the Government. Reith had to admit that the BBC did not have complete independence.

In 1927, the BBC became a corporation and Reith received a knighthood. There began a long period when, under Reith, the BBC became a very powerful and influential organisation. Reith himself said the BBC's purpose could be summed up in three words – *inform, educate, entertain.*

He wanted the BBC to be very different from all the many broadcasters in the USA who relied on advertising and cheap music. The BBC did indeed broadcast plenty of music but it was mostly opera and classical with some of what he called 'pop' music. Two early programmes, both of which lasted for decades, were *Woman's Hour* and *Children's Hour.*

To set what he felt was the right tone Reith chose public-school, university educated men to read the *News* wearing a dinner jacket and bow tie. He also set up a committee under the Poet Laureate to advise on what he called 'the correct pronunciation of the English tongue'. This led to the spread of 'public-school English'.

One area that was going to have great influence in the future, but which Reith did not like, was television. The centrepiece of his BBC remained the radio even into the 1950s and even the 1960s. As a listener said, 'The radio was on all the time, it was part of the background of family life, something we all shared.'

John Gunther, the American author, famous for his *Inside* stories, wrote that Reith's 'modernist citadel on Portland

Place is more important in the life of Britain than most government offices. He rules the BBC with a hand of granite and has made it probably the finest broadcasting organisation in the world.'

In 1948 the BBC began an annual series called the Reith Lectures whose aim was to advance 'public understanding and debate about significant issues of contemporary interest'.

Another area where Reith was not in agreement with most of the British population was in his admiration for both of the European dictators of the 1920s and 1930s, Benito Mussolini and Adolf Hitler. Entertaining Marconi in 1935 he said: 'I have always admired Mussolini immensely and constantly hailed him as the outstanding example of accomplishing high democratic purpose by means which, though not democratic, were the only possible ones.'

Of Hitler he wrote in his diary: 'I really admire the way Hitler has cleaned up what looked like an incipient revolt against him by the Brown Shirt leaders.'

In other words, Reith admired strong leadership and lack of tolerance of anyone who disagreed with them. He carried that through at the BBC if not quite to the same extent as Mussolini and Hitler!

31. FRANCIS CRICK

Francis Crick, with the American James Watson, was the biologist who discovered the structure of DNA.

Born near Northampton in 1916, he was educated at Mill Hill School and University College London from where he graduated in physics in 1937. When the Second World War broke out in September 1939 he became a member of the Admiralty's mine design department. It was while he was in this department that he decided that his real interest was biology not physics. In 1947, having decided to enter some field of biological research he secured a research studentship from the Medical Research Council and joined the Strangeways Institute in Cambridge which specialised in research in cell biology.

In 1949 he joined M.F. Perutz and J.C. Kendrew in Cambridge's Cavendish Laboratory as a member of the Medical Research Council Unit which developed into the Medical Research Council Laboratory of Molecular Biology. He remained a member for the rest of his career.

His major discovery, which came in 1953, was the double-helical structure of deoxyribonucleic acid or DNA. This was the substance in almost every living cell which is the repository of the hereditary information that determines the characteristics of the organism. Legend has it that they burst into the bar in the Eagle pub in Benet Street in Cambridge and announced that they had 'discovered the secret of life' and had the proof in their lab.

The discovery of the double-helix structure of DNA was recognised as the most important single contribution of the 20th century to fundamental biology and Crick (and Watson) became internationally recognised. Crick, Watson and Wilkins (who had carried out some of the initial experimental work) were awarded the Nobel Prize for Medicine in 1962. If she had still been alive (and perhaps if she had been a man), Rosalind Franklin would also have been included in recognition of her contribution.

In spite of this success, the structure of DNA was not the only contribution to science made by Crick. He was

also responsible for the formation of the so-called 'central dogma' that biological information, stored in nucleic acid and passed on by replication, is transformed into protein molecules, but that the reverse transformation never occurs.

He also played a leading part in the work that led to the elucidation in detail of the genetic code by means of which biological information is recorded. He was largely responsible for several concepts underlying the understanding of the mechanism by which biological information is translated into protein molecules, especially the idea of a 'messenger' carrying information from one part of the cell to another, and for the 'adapter hypothesis' which explains the way in which specific protein molecules corresponding to that information are assembled. Both of these fundamental concepts were confirmed by experiment.

Crick was recognised by colleagues as an outstanding scientist with deeper mathematical and physical insight than any contemporary in the field of science. He was an atheist who felt the mysterious phenomena of life could be explained, not by the existence of some god, but in terms of physics and chemistry. Crick became a fellow of the new Churchill College with its emphasis on science in the late 1950s and was totally against the College having a chapel, saying, 'This is supposed to be a college for the 21st century. We don't need all that mumbo-jumbo.'

After much discussion a chapel was built and Crick resigned his fellowship. This is what he said about Christianity: 'I do not respect Christian beliefs. I think they are ridiculous. If we could get rid of them we could more easily get down to the serious problem of trying to find out what the world is all about.'

For someone who did not believe in the after-life Crick

certainly achieved immortality not only in his discoveries but in the influence he had on other scientists.

30. GREG DYKE

Greg Dyke has been selected as one of the *50 Most Influential Britons of the Last 100 Years* not because of his time as Director-General of the BBC but thanks to his part in establishing football's Premier League.

The Premier League, through its resultant, constant and unrelenting coverage on television, and the huge sums of money involved, not least the salaries of the players, has changed the British public's enthusiasm for football out of all recognition.

The attendances at the games in all four leagues of the Football Association were very high in the 1940s and early 1950s as people were anxious to enjoy entertainment again after the privations and scarce opportunities for watching games during the Second World War. However, from the mid-1950s, especially as the ownership of televisions became virtually universal, crowds at professional football matches declined and reached a low point in the 1980s.

In 1990 Greg Dyke, who was Managing Director of London Weekend Television at the time, met representatives of the 'Big Five' football clubs in England. The 'Big Five' were Manchester United, Arsenal, Liverpool, Tottenham Hotspur and Everton. No Chelsea! This meeting led to the break away from the Football League. Dyke's suggestion was that it would be better if only the best and largest clubs were featured on television and that such clubs should have a larger share of the television rights money.

The Football Association, which did not enjoy a good relationship with the existing Football League, thought the possible break-away league was a good idea.

ITV offered £205 million and then £262 million (about £650 million today) for the television rights but were outbid by Rupert Murdoch whose recently purchased Sky Television was losing money. Apparently, Alan Sugar, Chairman of Tottenham Hotspur at the time, was heard to say to Murdoch on the telephone, 'Blow them out of the water.'

The Premier League was founded on 27 May 1992. Initially there were going to be only 18 clubs to alleviate fixture congestion. The Football Association was persuaded that this reduction to 18 would help the England team. In the event, there were 22 inaugural members in the League: Arsenal, Aston Villa, Blackburn Rovers, Chelsea, Coventry City, Crystal Palace, Everton, Ipswich Town, Leeds United, Liverpool, Manchester City, Manchester United, Middlesbrough, Norwich City, Nottingham Forest, Oldham Athletic, Queens Park Rangers, Sheffield United, Sheffield Wednesday, Southampton, Tottenham Hotspur, Wimbledon.

By the start of the 2015/16 season only eleven of those teams were still in the Premier League, seven were in the Championship, three in the First Division (what was called the Third Division in the 1980s and earlier) and finally, Wimbledon in the Second (now the Fourth) Division.

In 1995, the number of teams in the Premier League was reduced to 20 when 4 teams were relegated to, and only 2 promoted from, the *Championship* league.

One of the main results of the foundation of the Premier League was how it internationalised football at this, its highest level.

First, many of the clubs were bought by foreigners, especially Americans who were keen to get their hands on the television rights money. Second, there were many European managers and finally, and perhaps most worryingly in terms of the England football team, the number of overseas players increased sharply so that, by the start of the 2015/16 season, the number of overseas players amounted to over 70 per cent of the team.

There have been many sponsors of the League so it has had a number of different names:

1993–2001	FA Carling Premiership
2001–2004	Barclaycard Premiership
2004–2007	Barclays Premiership
2007–2015	Barclays Premier League

By 2015 it was an unusual Englishman who expressed no interest in football and virtually everyone supported a team whether it was a local one or elsewhere.

Greg Dyke has had other important jobs most notably Director-General of the BBC from 2000 to 2004 where he famously said he would cut the 'crap' and reduce administration costs from 24 per cent to 15 per cent of total income, but it is his part in the creation of the Premier League where he had his greatest influence.

29. GALTON AND SIMPSON

Ray Galton and Alan Simpson changed comedy on radio and television in Britain for all time. Considering their background and how they met, this was an amazing feat.

They met in a sanatorium in Surrey in 1948 when both

were suffering from tuberculosis and were not expected to live for long (both are still alive 67 years later!). This is what Galton said of their meeting:

> When Alan went past, the room went dark, because he was a big man – about 6ft 4in and 18 or 19 stone. I saw this shuffling figure with a big, brown dressing gown on, with the collar turned up … Who the hell's that? I thought, because you expect everyone in a sanatorium to be thin and weedy, and he was the biggest guy I'd ever seen.

They hit it off together and gradually began to write comedy. Eventually, they recovered from their tuberculosis and were introduced to Dennis Main Wilson at the BBC. Between them they devised a programme, *Hancock's Half Hour*, which would change the course of British situation comedy forever. It would follow the misadventures of a central character and his associates and would not have 'jokes'. The standard comic format of the time was typified by *The Goon Show*.

Hancock's Half Hour was launched on BBC radio in November 1954. The 'hero' was Anthony Aloysius St John Hancock, who felt he was misunderstood by the world and wasn't achieving the successes he thought he deserved.

The series lasted on the radio for seven years with over 100 episodes and ran concurrently with a television series from 1956. Other stars at the time who appeared in the radio series were: Bill Kerr, Kenneth Williams, Moira Lister, Andrée Melly and Hattie Jacques. Strongly featured was Sidney (Sid) James who also starred in the television series.

Unfortunately the real Hancock suffered from a number of character defects which meant he fell out with almost everyone including Galton and Simpson. He had already fallen out with Sid James who did not appear in the television shows after 1960. As it happens, two of Hancock's funniest and most remembered episodes, *The Radio Man* and *The Blood Donor* (many people can recite them word-for-word), were performed without Sid James.

Hancock's health declined (he became an alcoholic), his performances declined as a result and he committed suicide in Australia in 1968, at the age of only 44. The comedian Spike Milligan would say later, 'Very difficult man to get on with. He used to drink excessively. You felt sorry for him. He ended up on his own. I thought, he's got rid of everybody else, he is going to get rid of himself and he did.'

Nevertheless for a generation listening to radio and watching television in the 1950s he emptied the streets when *Hancock's Half Hour* was being broadcast.

And it was Galton and Simpson who wrote the scripts. Their other great and influential success was *Steptoe and Son*, of which four series were broadcast from 1962 to 1965 and another four series from 1970 to 1974. It was remade in the USA as *Sanford and Son*, in Sweden as *Albert & Herbert* and in the Netherlands as *Stiefbeen en Zoon*.

At its peak in the UK *Steptoe and Son* was watched by about 28 million people per episode. As with *Hancock's Half Hour* the stars were actors rather than comedians cracking jokes. The comedy was their tragic/comic approach to life. It took over from *Hancock* to become the benchmark by which all comedy on TV and radio was judged. The series won Galton and Simpson the Writer's Guild Award in 1962 and 1963.

Galton and Simpson won a lifetime achievement award from the Writer's Guild Award in 1997 and were awarded OBEs in 2000. They are acknowledged as the founding fathers of British situation comedy. As Christopher Stevens wrote in the *Introduction* to the book *The Masters of Sitcom*, 'Everything that's funniest in sitcom history had its beginning with Galton and Simpson. They didn't only invent the genre, they created the characters whose genes would be passed down through all the classic sitcoms.'

28. NUFFIELD

What Lord Nuffield, born William Morris in October 1877, achieved in the motor car industry was remarkable. He was born in a terraced house in Worcester but moved with his family to Oxford when he was three. He left school at fifteen and became an apprentice to a local bicycle seller and repairer. When he was sixteen he set up his own bicycle repairing business in a shed in the garden of his family home. As it was reasonably successful he opened a shop in the Oxford High Street, assembling as well as repairing bicycles. He also raced his own model of bicycle, called The Morris, and became champion of Oxford, Berkshire and Buckinghamshire.

In 1901 he began to work with motorcycles and, in 1902 bought buildings in Longwall Street from which he repaired bicycles but also operated a taxi service and sold, repaired and hired cars. He became an agent for various makes of cars, some of which did not survive very long, such as Arrol-Johnston, Belsize and Hupmobile, and others which did survive and flourish in the first half of the 20th century, such as Humber, Singer, Standard and Wolseley.

He expanded and in 1910 built new premises, described as The Oxford Motor Palace. He adopted a new name, *The Morris Garage* (the start of what became the famous MG sports car).

In 1912, Morris designed his first car, the Bullnose Morris. His ambition was to produce a popular car which would bring motoring to many and not just the rich. He bought in many of the components, including engines and axles from the USA, and began constructing the cars in a disused military training college in Cowley, a suburb of Oxford. The Morris Oxford was announced at the 1912 Motor Show and the first car produced in April 1913. The big competitor was Ford but every Ford at that stage was imported and Morris felt there had to be room for a British manufacturer.

The first Morris Oxford was a two-seater, 8.9 horsepower car and was priced at £165 (about £16,500 today). It was not the cheapest on the market but Morris was determined to concentrate on quality and reliability. A thousand were built in 1914 alone.

During the First World War, his factory produced munitions but, in 1919, car production resumed. In that year Morris manufactured 387 cars. By 1925 annual production reached 56,000 or over 1,000 a week and in the six years from 1919 to 1925 he either built or purchased factories in Abingdon, Birmingham and Swindon.

In 1927 Morris paid £730,000 (about £40 million today) for assets of Wolseley Motors Limited which had collapsed. The following year he launched the Morris Minor which was based on Wolseley's overhead camshaft 8hp car. This was followed in 1929 by the MG Midget.

During the 1920s he bought components companies including Hotchkiss, which was making his American engines under licence. He also bought the back-axle

manufacturer E.G. Wrigley, and SU Carburettors, and in the 1930s he bought Riley, manufacturer of the Riley car.

Also during the 1920s, Ford began production at Dagenham in Essex and the giant American car manufacturer General Motors bought Vauxhall and began production in Britain in Luton. When shares on Wall Street plunged in October 1929 bringing on a world depression which lasted into the 1930s, the car industry suffered with all other industries. For example in the UK in 1931 registrations for 12hp cars dropped from 26,000 to 17,000 and this was especially serious for Morris Motors whose 11.9hp Cowley was still its bread and butter line.

Morris concentrated on his Morris Minors and the popularity of these helped him weather the storm. He also worked hard to build up his export sales. An importer from Portugal, A.M. Almeida, visited Cowley and later said of Morris, 'My immediate impression was that here was a man who, despite natural simplicity of manner, was a strong-minded man of resolute opinion, interested in the smallest details and resolved to improve the production of his cars. He took notes of everything.'

During the 1930s exports from Cowley grew so that the 12 per cent of production from Cowley going overseas in 1933 became 21 per cent in the period 1937 to 1939. In 1939 Cowley produced its millionth car.

During the Second World War Morris concentrated on manufacturing the tools of war as he had done in the First World War but in 1945 he returned to cars and prospered in what became a sellers' market as the world became gradually more prosperous.

In 1952 Morris, by then Lord Nuffield, agreed to merge his Morris Motors with the Austin Motor Company to form The British Motor Corporation Limited or BMC as it became known. It meant that the new company had 39 per cent of British output producing a wide range of cars, commercial vehicles and agricultural tractors under the brand names Austin, Morris, MG, Austin-Healey, Riley and Wolseley. In 1968 BMC merged with Leyland Motors to become British Leyland Motor Corporation (BLMC).

Competition, lack of good new design and appalling labour relations led to a sharp decline in BLMC's fortunes in the 30 years after 1970 but this does not detract from the influence William Morris had on the British motor industry from 1912 to 1952. His strengths were his careful commercial practice and costing policy. He was an instinctive salesman and publicist and said, 'From the first I set out to cater for the man-in-the-street, the potential large class of enthusiastic but not too well-off drivers.'

After work his main interest was charity and, after selling many of his shares, he founded Nuffield College in Oxford and the Nuffield Foundation. He also founded BUPA (British United Provident Association) in 1947. In terms of honours he was made an OBE in 1917, a Baronet in 1929, a Baron in 1934 and a Viscount in 1938.

27. JACK COHEN

Tesco's founder, Jack Cohen, was born in the East End of London and grew up in Whitechapel. His family was Jewish, his father a Polish immigrant. He was named Jacob Edward Kohen but was known as Jack from an early age and indeed later changed his name to John Edward Cohen in 1930 at the request of his bank manager because of all the other Jacob

Cohens banking with the Midland's branch in Hackney. He went to the local council school until he was fourteen when he left to become an apprentice tailor working for his father. In 1917 he joined the Royal Flying Corps and served in France, Egypt and Palestine. He was on board a ship sunk by a mine offshore from Alexandria and returned to England after contracting malaria.

Cohen was reluctant to go back into tailoring and opened a market stall in Hackney selling surplus NAAFI (Navy, Army and Air Force Institutes) stock he had bought with his £30 demob money (£1,800 today). He had been able to get a job in the City enabling him to save. He took £4 and made a profit of £1 on the first day. He expanded to have a number of market stalls and also started a wholesale business. He soon realised he made a good salesman and put it down to his natural qualities of self-confidence and cheek, good humour, perseverance and a loud voice. He and his wife, whom he married in 1924, worked seven days a week starting at dawn and counting the takings until late in the evening. In 1924 he created the TESCO brand. The name came from the initials of his main supplier, T.E. Stockwell and the first two letters of his surname. By 1929 his turnover was £29,000 (£1.75million today). In 1931 he abandoned the market stalls and opened the first two high street shops – without doors – in Becontree and Burnt Oak. By 1939 there were 100 Tesco stores.

Although the early 1930s were economically grim all over the world following the Wall Street Crash in 1929, gradually things became better with the new industries of electricals, chemicals and motor cars leading to the building of new factories and large housing estates. Jack Cohen was keen to cash in and his daughter Shirley said later, 'We'd be going along and suddenly he'd say "This looks a good place for a shop!" and he'd leap out and chat a few people up.'

Tesco prospered in the Second World War as it sold goods everyone wanted at prices most grocers would not entertain. After the War, Cohen visited the USA and was struck with the potential of the supermarkets when he saw the success of Safeway, Food Fair and Atlantic & Pacific with their bright and spacious isles stocked with attractively packaged groceries. Customers piled their goods on to trolleys and paid at the checkout. He was told that about half of the food retailers were self-service but had 80 per cent of the grocery sales. Cohen returned to the UK to see if the system would work there.

His early experience of self-service at a store in St Albans was not entirely successful, first because of pilfering and second because middle-class women did not easily accept the idea of filling their own baskets rather than have someone do it for them. Nevertheless, by 1950 there were 20 Tesco self-service stores and, by 1959, there were 185 Tesco stores of which 140 were self-service.

There followed the major battle of Cohen's career, the fight against Resale Price Maintenance. Eventually, he won when Edward Heath abolished it. During the 1960s Tesco went completely national, largely through a number of takeovers including Victor Value, so that by the end of the decade Tesco had no fewer than 834 self-service stores.

Jack Cohen was knighted in 1969 and continued to work at building Tesco even into his seventies. Hyman Kreitman, his son-in-law, and a key participant in the building of Tesco, said, 'Although Sir John has relinquished his office of Joint Chairman he has not retired. He attends the office daily and participates in our policy discussions, playing an active part in the company's affairs.'

And Ian, later Lord, MacLaurin, one of Tesco's most successful Chief Executives, said:

He came into my office – this old man, this wonderful old man with his worn-out face – and he got hold of my lapels and he shook me and he said, 'It's all your bloody idea and if it fails you know what's going to happen to you', and I said, 'Guvnor, I know what's going to happen to me.'

Dame Shirley Porter said her father never sat still. She recalled the tie pins he had made:

YCDBSOYA: you can't do business sitting on your arse. He used to give them to prime ministers, anybody and everybody. He would not have got on in politics because he couldn't keep his mouth closed: he would say what he felt and be difficult. He could really lose his temper. He would be very sorry about it afterwards. If he had any politics at all, it was YCDBSOYA. He believed in people and hard work. He believed in doing things for yourself and he was very, very family-minded.

The growth of Tesco can be charted as follows:

1919   Jack Cohen sets out a stall on a hired barrow in Well Street, Hackney
1924   Cohen sells TESCO tea
1932   Tesco incorporated at Companies House
1934   Tesco HQ established at Angel Road, Edmonton and first warehouse built
1947   Public listing on London Stock Exchange
1949   First self-service Tesco store opens in St Albans, Hertfordshire
1956   First Tesco supermarket opens in Maldon, Essex
1957   Tesco acquires 70 stores and restaurants in London and south-east from Williamsons Ltd
1958   150 Tesco stores offer self-service

1963	Launch of Green Shield stamps in Tesco stores
1966	51 stores open in one year. *Financial Times* puts Tesco top of UK company growth league
1968	Victor Value acquired and Crawley Superstore opens with 40,000 square feet of selling space
1973	Tesco shares bought for £75 in 1947 now worth £6,000
1974	Turnover exceeds £500 million (multiply by 20 for today's value)
1995	Tesco overtakes Sainsbury's market share
2005	Tesco profits exceed £2 billion
2012	Tesco operating in fourteen countries serving 50 million customers a week and employing 500,000 people.

26. ELIZABETH DAVID

To understand Elizabeth David's contribution and influence in the world of food in Britain we need to realise the state of food in Britain at the beginning of the 1950s.

Since 1939 many food items had been rationed. For example bacon went on ration in January 1940 and only came off ration in July 1954, ham also went on ration in January 1940 and came off in October 1952, other meat suffered rationing for the same period as bacon, cheese was on ration from May 1941 until May 1954 and even sugar was rationed from January 1940 until September 1953.

David wrote in her *French Country Cooking*, published in 1951, 'Rationing, the disappearance of servants, and the bad and expensive meals served in restaurants, have led

English women to take a far greater interest in food than was formerly considered polite.'

She wanted food and its preparation to become important in women's lives saying:

> Some sensible person once remarked that you spend the whole of your life either in your bed or in your shoes. Having done the best you can by shoes and bed, devote all the time and resources at your disposal to the building up of a fine kitchen. It will be, as it should be, the most comforting, and comfortable, room in the house.

She came from an aristocratic and wealthy background. Her father was a Conservative Member of Parliament for Eastbourne and her mother the daughter of Viscount Ridley. At sixteen she was sent from her English boarding school to study French literature at the Sorbonne and lived for eighteen months with a French family who were keen on their food and who showed Elizabeth David how dull British food was.

After a spell trying to be an actress in the 1930s she sailed to Greece in July 1939 with her lover, Charles Gibson-Cowan. On the way, they stayed in Antibes in the south of France where she met the author Norman Douglas. He inspired her about the Mediterranean and the importance of good food. As she said later, he taught her to 'search out the best, insist on it, and reject all that was bogus and second-rate.'

David and Gibson-Cowan were forced to flee from Greece when the German army invaded and they spent most of the war in Egypt. After marriage and a spell in India, David returned to England where she encountered the post-war austerity as well as, in her opinion, terrible food: 'There was flour and water soup seasoned solely with pepper; bread and gristle rissoles; dehydrated onions and carrots; corned beef toad in the hole. I need not go on.'

She began writing articles on Mediterranean cookery which were published in 1949 in *Harper's Bazaar*. She put them into a book called *A Book of Mediterranean Food* and offered it to a number of publishers all of whom turned it down. After some modification it was eventually accepted by John Lehmann who paid her an advance of £100 (about £3,000 today) and *A Book of Mediterranean Food* with illustrations by John Minton was published in 1950.

It proved to be a great success and David quickly followed up with *French Country Cooking*, published in 1951, *Italian Food* 1954 and *Summer Cooking* 1955. In 1956 she began to write for the *Sunday Times, Vogue* and *House & Garden*. In 1960 *French Provincial Cooking* was published and received rave reviews. *The Times Literary Supplement* wrote:

> *French Provincial Cooking* needs to be read rather than referred to quickly. It discourses at some length the type and origin of the dishes popular in various French regions, as well as the culinary terms, herbs and kitchen equipment used in France. But those who can give the extra to this book will be well repaid by dishes such as *La Bourride de Charles Bérot* and *Cassoulet Colombié.*

The Observer wrote that it was difficult to think of any home that could do without the book and described David as 'a very special kind of genius'.

Her achievements in educating the British about the possibilities of good and interesting food were recognised by her being awarded an OBE in 1976, followed by a CBE in 1986. She was also made Chevalier du Mérite Agricole.

25. SIR FRANK WHITTLE

The jet engine transformed both peaceful air travel and war in the air and the man most responsible for its invention and development is Frank, later Sir Frank, Whittle.

Born in June 1907 in Coventry, Whittle grew up acquiring engineering skills from his father who was a practical engineer and mechanic. He was determined to join the newly formed Royal Air Force and passed the entrance exam with a high mark at the age of sixteen. However, he was rejected on medical grounds because he was only five feet tall and had a small chest measurement. He built up his chest and reapplied when he was taller but was rejected again. Undeterred, he tried once more under an assumed name and this time got into the School of Technical Training at RAF Cranwell.

In 1928 he produced a thesis, *Future Developments in Aircraft Design*. In it he showed that a high altitude aircraft could fly faster because of the reduced air resistance and that 'the turbine is the most efficient prime mover known so it is possible it will be developed for aircraft, especially if some means of driving it by petrol could be devised'.

As Andrew Nahum pointed out in his book *Frank Whittle, Invention of the Jet*:

The gas turbine, in a heavy, industrial and relatively inefficient form, already existed and was employed in industrial plants where a cheap supply of combustible gas was available. For example, from 1914 the Thyssen company installed them at several steelworks in Germany where they ran on waste blast furnace gas.

However, the jet propulsion idea made the Whittle gas

turbine/jet engine conceptually different from the propeller turbine, in which as much energy as possible is extracted as rotary shaft horsepower from the exhaust by the turbine stages. Whittle's idea instead left as much energy as possible in the gas stream to form a high velocity exhaust jet. This simplification of the gas turbine made Whittle's jet proposal attractive for development at a time when the combined inefficiencies of the compressor, the turbine and the required reduction gearing and propeller drive seemed, in aggregate, too great to make a propeller turbine unit viable.

Whittle asked himself, 'Why not substitute a turbine for the piston engine?'

He felt that, instead of using a piston engine to provide the compressed air for the burner, a turbine could be used to extract some power from the exhaust and drive a similar compressor to those used for superchargers. The remaining exhaust would power the aircraft.

In 1929 Whittle sent his concept to the Air Ministry but was turned down. However, a Flying Officer, formerly a patent examiner, suggested he patent the idea, which he did.

Not much further happened until 1935 when Whittle was introduced to two investment bankers at O.T. Falk & Partners, and one of them, Lancelot Law Whyte, said:

The impression he made was overwhelming. I have never been so quickly convinced, or so happy to find one's highest standard met ... This was genius, not talent. Whittle expressed his idea with superb conciseness: 'Reciprocating engines are exhausted. They have hundreds of parts jerking to and fro, and they cannot be made more powerful without becoming complicated. The engine of the future must produce 2,000 hp with one moving part: a spinning turbine and compressor.

Falk & Partners financed a new company, Power Jets Ltd, which entered into an agreement with steam turbine specialists, British Thomson-Houston, to build an experimental engine facility at a BTH factory near Rugby.

Financial problems continued to delay progress and it was not until January 1940 (four months into the Second World War) that the Air Ministry finally placed a contract with the Gloster Aircraft Company for an aircraft to test the Whittle Supercharger W1.

Finally on 12 April 1941 a W1 powered aircraft took off at RAF Cranwell. It flew for seventeen minutes and reached a speed of 340 mph. At the end of this successful flight a colleague said to Whittle, 'Frank, it flies,' to which Whittle replied, 'Well, that's what it was bloody well designed to do, wasn't it?'

In terms of mass production of Whittle's engines he was involved with Rover for a time but then he was introduced to Rolls-Royce who were already mass-producing the Merlin engines that had been so successful powering the Spitfire and Hurricane in the Battle of Britain. Rolls-Royce gradually took over production of Whittle's engine and Ernest, later Lord, Hives, Managing Director of Rolls-Royce, became convinced that the company's future lay with the jet engine. He was quite correct.

24. DR BEECHING

Dr, later Baron, Beeching had a dramatic effect on the lives of the majority of Britons with his report *The Reshaping of British Railways*, published on 27 March 1963.

It called for the closure of no less than one-third of the country's 7,000 railway stations, and the removal of passenger services from around 5,000 miles of existing routes.

The rail transport system had grown from zero to a complete coverage of the country in the nineteenth century, built by a number of private companies. However, it was nationalised in 1948 under the Labour Government's nationalisation programme.

Prompting Beecham's report was the fact that the existing railway system was highly complicated and inefficient and losing millions of pounds a year. In 1961 it was calculated to be losing £300,000 (nearly £1 million today) every day. Its traffic was also declining in terms of both passengers and goods due to the growth of motor traffic. For example, one third of the network was carrying one per cent of the traffic and, of 18,000 passenger coaches, 6,000 were only used 18 times a year or less. The system was costing £3 million to £4 million a year (£75 million to £100 million today) to maintain and earning only £0.5 million (£12.5 million today).

The closures were carried out from 1963 to 1970 and were heavily criticised, especially of course by those affected.

Another explosion of criticism was caused by the salary paid to Beeching as the First Chairman of the British Railways Board. He was paid £24,000 a year (about £600,000 today) which was the same as he had been receiving as a director of ICI (Imperial Chemical Industries). This was £14,000 more than the Prime Minister, Harold Macmillan, and two and a half times more than any head of a nationalised industry at the time.

Needless to say, the cuts meant loss of jobs and there was plenty of opposition from the trade unions. Beeching was unrepentant, saying, 'I suppose I'll be looked upon as the axe man, but it was surgery, not mad chopping.'

And, as well as cuts, there was also some modernisation carried out as a result of Beeching's report. For example, there was a greater emphasis on block trains, a rail cargo shipping method whereby all the storage cars were shipped from the same point and arrived at the same destination, which did not require expensive and time-consuming shunting en route.

After all the drama of the first Beeching Report, he produced a second one in February 1965. This time he said that of the 7,500 miles of trunk railway throughout Britain only 3,000 miles 'should be selected for future development' and therefore have further investment.

The achievements and long-term influence of Richard Beeching were very well summarised in the biography written by R.H.N. Hardy, a railway manager himself. He wrote:

Richard Beeching became a remarkable, indeed an outstanding, Chairman of the Board and leader of the railway industry … his famous Reshaping Report was constructive and for us within the system, his work changed our thinking, our methods of doing things, our ideas on assessment of managers and our systems – such as they were – of financial control. He was a great believer in forward planning but, in the railway industry, he went further than that and his influence is felt to this day …

… if it was by bringing to the attention of the country the critical situation facing the railways and the taxpayer, if it was to make the public face up to the question of striking a balance between the social need for public transport where it could not pay its way and the financial burden on the community if it were to be provided, if it was to create a basic internal organisation that stood the test of time for many years, then he succeeded and succeeded magnificently.

23. SIR HENRY ROYCE

Henry Royce, the partner of Charles Rolls in the foundation of Rolls-Royce Ltd, was influential not only for the development of the Rolls-Royce cars but, more importantly, for the development of Rolls-Royce aero engines.

Rolls-Royce Ltd was founded in 1904 to produce cars and, as is well known, the company was soon producing what became known by many as 'the best car in the world'. However, the future of the company was thrown into jeopardy by the outbreak of the First World War on 4 August 1914. At the first board meeting after the outbreak of war, Claude Johnson, the Managing Director, was authorised 'to reduce the works wages to about one fourth by discharging about half the hands and allowing the remainder to work only half time'. More surprisingly, the board decided that the company 'would not avail itself of the opportunity, now possibly arising, of making or assembling aero engines for the British Government'.

This decision was soon reversed and Henry Royce began to develop his first aero engine. On the outbreak of the War not a single British aero engine was in production. The country was still totally dependent on France for them. Rapid progress was made and, by August 1915, Royce's engine was being tested. Once proven, Government orders flowed in for the engine, named the *Eagle,* and Rolls-Royce engineers were sent to the USA to supervise an extra 1,500 engines that were being built there.

The *Eagle* was soon followed by the *Hawk* engine and then the *Falcon* which became the standard engine for the British Fighter F2B, Britain's most effective fighter of the First

World War. It could dive faster than any other fighter and it was often able to fly home even when severely damaged. With the *Falcon* it became a byword for reliability. Finally, before the end of the War, Rolls-Royce manufactured the *Condor* which was fitted into the Handley Page bombers as they wanted maximum horsepower in a twin-engine design.

The next exciting development once the First World War was over was the flight across the Atlantic by Alcock and Brown in their Vimy aircraft. The Vickers Vimy was powered by two of Rolls-Royce's *Eagle VIIIs*.

The next triumph came with the Schneider Trophy which was an international award presented to the nation with the fastest seaplane over a pre-determined, measured course. There had been two contests before the First World War, none during the War and then the contests resumed in the 1920s with the Americans becoming dominant. Reg Mitchell, who went on to design the Spitfire, was busy designing aircraft to try and win the Schneider Trophy and he chose Rolls-Royce engines for the 1929 contest.

The engine they used was the *Kestrel* which Rolls-Royce had begun to develop in 1924. The *Kestrel* became the critical engine in re-establishing Rolls-Royce's position as the premier supplier of aero engines to the RAF. The *Kestrel* proved to be a fine forerunner of the *Merlin* engine which made Rolls-Royce world famous.

The engine supplied for the three successive British victories in the Schneider Trophy contest in 1929, 1930 and 1931 was referred to as the 'R' engine. One of Sir Henry Royce's last decisions was to authorise the development of a new engine bigger than the *Kestrel* incorporating as much 'R' technology as possible. This new engine was called the *Merlin* and as Gordon (son of Reginald) Mitchell said, 'The decision to fit the *Merlin* engine into Mitchell's type 300 fighter was a vital turning point in the development of the Spitfire.'

The *Merlin* powered not only the Supermarine Spitfire but also the Hawker Hurricane, the two magnificent fighter aircraft that enabled the RAF to defeat the German Luftwaffe in the Battle of Britain in 1940 and prevent a German invasion of Britain.

Initially, in the Battle of Britain which began in the summer of 1940, the Spitfires and Hurricanes were powered by *Merlin IIIs*. As the battle went into the autumn a number of Spitfires were fitted with the *Merlin XII*, which gave enhanced altitude performance. Later in the Hurricane II, the *Merlin XX* was fitted, with its improved supercharger intake design and two-speed supercharger. Production of the *Merlin* engine was increased from 2,000 in 1939 to 7,000 in 1940.

Royce's *Merlin* engines may not have ultimately won the Second World War but they undoubtedly enabled Britain to escape losing it in 1940.

22. SIR DAVID ATTENBOROUGH

The fact that the President of the United States of America, Barack Obama, interviewed Sir David Attenborough in early 2015 shows how important Sir David's influence has been in explaining the natural world, not only to Britons but to people in other countries as well.

He was born in 1926 in Isleworth, west London and grew up in Leicester where his father was principal of University

College. He was interested in nature from an early age and collected fossils, stones and other natural specimens. He was educated at Wyggeston Grammar School for Boys in Leicester and won a scholarship to Clare College, Cambridge where he studied geology and zoology, leaving with a degree in natural sciences.

David joined the BBC in 1952 and was soon working on an animal programme with the naturalist Julian Huxley. His first television appearance was in *Zoo Quest*, and he began to travel the world with the second series of *Zoo Quest* filmed in South America where David could be seen in bushes and poking around anthills and armadillos' burrows.

David was diverted from his nature exploration when he became Controller of BBC Two in 1965, although he insisted on having a clause in his contract that would allow him to make programmes, and later that year he filmed elephants in Tanzania and, in 1969, made a three-part series on the cultural history of the Indonesian island of Bali. In 1971 he joined the first Western expedition to a remote highland valley in New Guinea to try and find a lost tribe.

Meanwhile he did a magnificent job at BBC Two establishing a wide portfolio of programmes on music, the arts, archaeology, travel, drama, sport, business science and natural history. One of his best decisions was to commission a thirteen-part series on the history of Western art. *Civilisation* won great acclaim when it was launched in 1969.

In that year David was promoted to Director of Programmes which meant he was responsible for the output of both BBC One and BBC Two. This was purely an administrative job and when he was put forward as a possible Director-General of the BBC in 1972 he decided that he would rather return to full-time programming on the subject that he really loved, natural history.

He became a freelance broadcaster and his next series was called *Eastwards with Attenborough*. He moved on to make *Life on Earth, The Tribal Eye, The Explorers* and for children, *Fabulous Animals*. *Life on Earth* became a huge success as was his next series, *The Living Planet*, which explored the adaptation of living things to their environment, and brought large international sales for the BBC.

Then, in 1990, David produced *The Trials of Life* which looked at animal behaviour through the different stages of life. It excited viewers with its sequences of killer whales hunting sea lions on a Patagonian beach and chimpanzees hunting and violently killing a colobus monkey. He then moved on to birds, producing *The Life of Birds* in 1998.

In his *The Life of Mammals*, produced in 2002, low-light and infrared cameras were used to show the behaviour of nocturnal mammals. The advances in macro photography allowed David to film the natural behaviour of very small animals and, in 2005, *Life in the Undergrowth* showed the world of invertebrates. He had now made programmes about nearly all the terrestrial animals and plants. To complete the set he made *Life in Cold Blood*, broadcast in 2008, which investigated reptiles and amphibians.

Still working in his eighties (now in 2015 he is 89) David looked back and said of *Life on Earth*:

There are some four million different kinds of animals and plants in the world. Four million different solutions to the problems of staying alive. This is the story of how a few of them came to be as they are … I've been lucky in my life to see some of the greatest spectacles that the natural world has to offer. Surely we have the responsibility to leave for future generations a planet that is healthy, inhabitable by all species.

Sir David Attenborough has certainly done that and his achievements and influence have been recognised throughout the world with comments such as 'the great communicator, the peerless educator' and 'the greatest broadcaster of our time'.

He has also collected many honorary titles, for example a knighthood and 31 degrees from British universities (more than any other person). In 2006 in a *Reader's Digest* poll he was named as the most trusted celebrity in Britain.

21. WINSTON CHURCHILL

Winston Churchill's outstanding characteristic was his determination to do what he thought was right irrespective of what his superiors, friends or allies might say or want. Thus, he crossed the floor of the House of Commons twice and resigned from the Conservative Shadow Cabinet as late as 1931 in protest against its attitude to India.

His great belief was the importance of Britain's place in the world. It was fitting for the elder son of Lord Randolph Churchill and grandson of the seventh Duke of Marlborough. Following a conventional upper class education at a preparatory school in Ascot and at Harrow public school, Churchill joined the British Army and served in India and North Africa, and South Africa in the Boer War. His inclination to criticise his senior officers led him wisely to leave the Army and pursue a career as a journalist and then as a politician. He also wrote a much acclaimed biography of his father.

In 1904 he left the Conservative Party, appalled by the protectionist approach of Joseph Chamberlain, and joined the Liberal Party. In 1908, when Asquith became Prime Minister, Churchill was promoted to the Cabinet and in that year married Clementine Hozier. He became close to Lloyd George as both promoted the new Liberalism, with Churchill strongly supporting Lloyd George's People's Budget of 1909.

As relations with Germany deteriorated Churchill was moved from Home Secretary to First Lord of the Admiralty and made every effort possible to build up the Royal Navy. At the beginning of the First World War in 1914 Churchill appointed Lord Fisher as Admiral of the Fleet and initially the two worked closely together to build up the fleet's supremacy over the German fleet. However, they fell out over how the fleet could have the greatest impact on the War. Fisher favoured the Baltic, Churchill the Dardanelles. Initially Churchill won the argument and an assault on the Dardanelles was planned. However, the implementation was faulty and the attack was repulsed with great loss of life. Unfairly, Churchill was blamed for the failure. He was forced to resign from the Cabinet.

After serving at the front, Churchill returned to London to become a close adviser of Lloyd George in the final months of the War in 1918. In the 1920s he became disillusioned with the Liberal Party and crossed the floor of the House of Commons to rejoin the Conservative Party in 1924. Much to his surprise he was appointed Chancellor of the Exchequer.

The major step in his first budget was a return to the Gold Standard. Many approved but Maynard Keynes, quite rightly, was critical. In retrospect, a revaluation upwards of the pound sterling was the last thing the British economy needed. In 1929, the Conservatives lost the General Election and Churchill was out of office for the following ten years though he was consistent in his warnings about Adolf Hitler and his urging of re-armament.

Churchill returned to office as First Lord of the Admiralty shortly after the Second World War broke out on 3 September 1939. Neville Chamberlain was Prime Minister but after the German takeover of Norway during which, as Peter Hennessy wrote in Never Again: Britain 1945–51, 'The deployment of British forces in Norway ... was chaotic in conception, confused in execution and humiliating in its outcome.'

Chamberlain was forced to resign and Churchill became Prime Minister.

The next two years were the greatest in Churchill's life when he undoubtedly rallied the British people to stand up to the ambition for world domination of the Nazi dictator, Adolf Hitler. On 13 May 1940 Churchill made perhaps his most famous, and certainly most quoted, speech, in which he said:

> I would say to the House, as I said to those who have joined this Government: I have nothing to offer but blood, toil, tears and sweat. We have before us an ordeal of the most grievous kind. We have before us many, many long months of struggle and of suffering.
>
> You ask what is our policy? I will say: It is to wage war, by sea, land and air, with all our might and with all the strength God can give us; to wage war against a monstrous tyranny, never surpassed in the dark, lamentable catalogue of human crime. That is our policy.
>
> You ask, what is our aim? I can answer in one word: it is victory, victory at all costs, victory in spite of all terror, victory, however long and hard the road may be, for without victory there is no survival.

In wartime Churchill was a great leader and his greatest contribution to the Allies' ultimate success in the War was his help in bringing the United States into the conflict and working closely with President Roosevelt until victory was achieved. However, in peacetime, by the time he was re-elected in 1951 after the British people had voted in a Labour Government in 1945, he was 77 years old and the achievements of the Conservative Government in the 1950s were effected by his younger colleagues.

20. JAMES DYSON

This is what Dyson wrote in 1997:

> It must have been some time in 1979 that I first heard the words, 'But, James, if there were a better kind of vacuum cleaner Hoover or Electrolux would have invented it.' That was when I left the first company I had set up – gave up security, income, and respectability – and persuaded an old friend to come in with me on a project I was developing in the pigsties behind my house.
>
> My experience was of a new kind of wheelbarrow, a high-speed launch craft, and a couple of castles in the air. For twelve years I laboured under heavier and heavier debt. I tried and failed to interest the major manufacturing companies in my product. I fought terrible legal battles to protect my vacuum cleaner. And in 1992 I went into production, on my own, as sole owner of the machine I had conceived, designed, built and tested alone.
>
> After hundreds of prototypes, thousands of modifications, and millions of tests, I was in terrible debt, but in love with

the Dual Cyclone. By 1997 I had a company turning over £100 million in the UK, and had generated sales of more than £1 billion worldwide. The Dyson was the biggest-selling vacuum cleaner in Britain. Bigger than Electrolux, bigger than Philips, bigger than Hoover. In 1996 my company became the first British manufacturer of domestic electrical goods to export to Japan.

By 2015 Dyson's business had worldwide sales of £1.5 billion and employed 6,000 people. Ninety per cent of sales are outside the UK. Dyson owns the entire company whose value is probably about £5 billion. Looking back to the foundation of the business, he spent five years in a coach house on a farm in the Cotswolds building no fewer than 5,127 prototypes before he was satisfied that his vacuum cleaner could be launched on the market.

And life for his family during those five years was not easy. His wife, Deirdre, had to work and she also had to accept that the bank had a charge on their house. Jake, Dyson's elder son, remembers his mother having to teach art to support them and said:

He would be in the cellar day after day, night after night, trying to form a perfect plastic cone [with a machine]. That's my most vivid memory – of him losing his rag each time it went wrong. But then I also remember when he came upstairs with a perfect one.

The Dyson company has sold more than 20 million of those vacuum cleaners.

In his vacuum cleaner he introduced cyclonic chambers which meant there was no need for a bag. He explains his technique of improvement as follows:

I've been inventing since college, and the process is pretty much always the same. You see some big problem – something that has a big Achilles' heel – and you can then proceed in one of two ways. You either develop a technology to solve the problem, or you happen to come across a technology that solves the problem. When you start, you really think you are going to get there quickly, and it always takes much longer than you ever thought.

When Dyson launched his 'G-Force' cleaner in 1983 no manufacturer or distributor would handle it as it killed the profitable market for replacement dust bags. Undeterred, Dyson launched it in Japan through catalogue sales and it won the 1991 International Design Fair prize in Japan. He had obtained his first US patent in 1986 and set up his own manufacturing company in 1993.

He promoted his cleaner on TV with the slogan 'Say goodbye to the bag' (at the time the market for bags was £100 million).

The Dyson Dual Cyclone became the fastest-selling cleaner not only in the UK but in the USA as well, though in the USA it was by value rather than volume. It outsold the cleaners of the companies that had rejected his idea.

Needless to say, other companies copied his cyclonic vacuum idea, including Hoover UK whom he sued for patent infringement and won about $5 million in damages.

Dyson continues to invent and develop new products some of which are commercially successful and some not, but it is his vacuum cleaner that has had the greatest success and most influence.

19. JOHN LOGIE BAIRD

Everyone knows that John Logie Baird invented television. This is a slight exaggeration. He was one of the inventors. Nevertheless, he undoubtedly contributed enough to have earned a place in this list.

In 2002 he was ranked 44th in the BBC's list of 100 Greatest Britons (of all time) after a UK-wide vote, and in 2006, he was named as one of the ten greatest Scottish scientists.

Television became a reality in January 1926 when John Logie Baird demonstrated the world's first television pictures. The images were sent from one side of a room to the other, mechanically scanned as 30 vertical strips of light which showed a head and shoulders picture of the person being televised. After a few years the development of electronic scanning and the cathode ray tube led to much higher resolution, but Baird's television system was the world's first and it stimulated research by the big radio conglomerates in Britain and the USA. Television was sent from London to Glasgow in 1927 and from London to New York in 1928.

Bizarrely, Baird had difficulty persuading the Director-General of the BBC, Sir John Reith, to allow the broadcasting of television. Baird had to have the co-operation of the BBC because it had a monopoly on public broadcasting at the time. It was not until 30 September 1929, after long negotiations, that Baird Television Ltd began to broadcast its programmes on an experimental basis using BBC medium wave facilities, but only after radio broadcasting had ended for the day at 11pm.

While these negotiations were proceeding Baird transmitted a long-distance television signal over 438

miles of telephone line between London and Glasgow and transmitted the world's first long-distance television pictures to the Central Hotel in Glasgow Central Station. In 1928 the Baird Television Development Company made the first transatlantic television transmission from London to Hartsdale, New York, and the first television programme for the BBC. In 1929 Baird and Bernard Natan founded France's first television company called Télévision-Baird-Natan. In 1931 Baird televised the first live transmission of the Epsom Derby.

Others were like Reith and did not like the idea of television. For example when Baird was seeking publicity to promote his invention he approached the *Daily Express*. The news editor did not want to know and apparently said to one of his staff, 'For God's sake, go down to reception and get rid of the lunatic who's down there. He says he's got a machine for seeing by wireless! Watch him – he may have a razor on him!'

Baird demonstrated the world's first colour transmission on 3 July 1928 using scanning discs at the transmitting and receiving ends with three spirals of apertures. In 1928 he also demonstrated stereoscopic television and, in 1932, he was the first person in the UK to demonstrate ultra-short wave transmission. (Ultra-short waves are now referred to as the VHF band.)

To begin with only one transmitter was available and the vision and sound signals had to be sent alternately. In March 1930 two transmitters were used so that vision and sound could be sent simultaneously.

In 1932 Baird Television was taken over by the Gaumont-British Picture Corporation which provided more finance for Baird to continue development. Baird himself, though he kept the title of Managing Director, no longer had any executive power and was restricted to research. There was a further setback for Baird in 1937 when the BBC adopted the Marconi-EMI-RCA electronic system of television in preference to Baird Television Ltd's system. Nevertheless Baird Television Ltd continued to operate successfully, making receivers and developing television for cinemas.

When the Second World War broke out in September 1939, television broadcasting stopped. Baird spent the War researching high-definition electronic colour television and stereoscopic television. Unfortunately, Baird was never very fit and, after spells in hospital during the War, he died at the relatively young age of 57 in 1946.

Although the development of television was made by a number of inventors most historians give credit to Baird for being the first to produce a live, moving greyscale television image from reflected light. He achieved this by obtaining a better photoelectric cell and improving the signal conditioning from the photocell and the video amplifier.

18. SIR MARCUS SIEFF

Marcus Sieff was Chairman of Marks & Spencer from 1972 to 1984 and had worked in the chain on and off since 1935, becoming a director in 1954, Assistant Managing Director in 1963, Vice-Chairman in 1965 and Joint Managing Director in 1967.

Marks & Spencer was founded by two penniless immigrants from Eastern Europe as a chain of penny bazaars in 1884. Ephraim Sieff established a business in Manchester sorting and re-selling cotton waste. Michael Marks borrowed £5

(about £500 today) to buy goods and sell them in villages around Leeds and Yorkshire. He set up a stall in the Leeds Market and used the slogan, 'Don't ask the price, it's a penny' (less than 50p today).

Michael established Marks & Spencer as a chain of penny bazaars in 1894. The chain expanded in the 1930s under the two principles of quality control and value for money, though just as important was staff welfare. Marcus Sieff argued that unhappy workers were inefficient workers and said, 'The development of good human relations in industry is very important. I use the term "good human relations in industry" rather than "industrial relations" because we are human beings at work, not industrial beings.'

The St Michael brand, in honour of Michael Marks, was introduced in 1928 and, by 1950, virtually all its goods were sold under that name. Like all retailers, M&S, or *Marks and Sparks* as it became known, had been forced to cope with rationing during the Second World War and into the 1950s, but the company was determined to show that fashion was not just for the rich. It put a great deal of effort into buying and selling clothing of improved quality and also durability.

In 1934 M&S had been the first retailer to set up its own research laboratory to pioneer new fabrics and, in 1948, it launched its own Food Technology department to work closely with suppliers, producers and farmers. In 1954 the research laboratory undertook the first systematic survey of women's leg sizes to create a new and improved sizing system for stockings.

M&S continued to expand in the 1950s and 1960s and became synonymous with good design, high quality and reasonable prices. It was 'the must' shop for the middle class. Marcus Sieff had joined the M&S board of directors in 1954. He was responsible for the food department which grew very fast under his leadership. Later he took charge of store operations and personnel.

Marcus Sieff reached the top of the group in the late 1960s and he insisted that M&S was an example of the best kind of free enterprise with a human face, something particularly relevant during the 1970s, which was a period of poor industrial relations with continuous strikes. He also fought against Government interference and high taxation and was at pains to publicise the fact that M&S bought 90 per cent of its merchandise from British manufacturers with whom the company always tried to foster a close relationship.

Sieff himself said, 'No Marks and Spencer could build up a company like ours from scratch under conditions prevailing today'.

Two years after he made this statement, Labour was voted out and Margaret Thatcher came to power, quickly providing him with a peerage and an approach to taxation more congenial to him.

The *Guardian* obituary of Marcus Sieff included this appraisal of his management:

Five years after assuming the Chairmanship, and with a Labour government in office, he claimed that general living standards were falling. There were, he said, three reasons. Initiative was being stifled through taxation policies, there was conflict between management, and free enterprise was being progressively destroyed. He argued that employees must share in the success of a company, but that the taxman took much of whatever he gave to his employees. M & S was finding it harder to recruit good people. Many preferred to go into the 'feather-bedded' government service, where they had a secure life and inflation-proof pension, which no company that had to 'earn its keep' could afford.

17. J.K. ROWLING

Born on 31 July 1965, J.K. Rowling is now world famous as the author of the *Harry Potter* series. By the middle of 2015 they had sold more than 400 million copies and the series was the best-selling book series in history. Furthermore, the film series based on the books also became collectively the highest-grossing in history.

Rowling was born into a reasonably prosperous middle-class family. Her father was an aircraft engineer working at Rolls-Royce in Bristol. Her mother was a science technician. The family lived in Yate, Gloucestershire but moved to a nearby village, Winterbourne, when Rowling was four. She went to St Michael's Primary School which, interestingly, was founded by slavery abolitionist William Wilberforce and education reformer Hannah More.

Rowling has a sister, Dianne, who is two years younger and she wrote fantasy stories as a child which she would read to this sister. When she was nine the family moved again, this time to Tutshill, near Chepstow in Wales. For her secondary education she went to Wyedean School and College where her mother worked in the science department.

Rowling did not enjoy her teenage years. Her mother was not in the best of health and Rowling fell out with her father. One thing from which she did benefit was a gift from a great aunt of Jessica Mitford's autobiography, *Hons and Rebels*. Mitford became a heroine to Rowling who proceeded to read all her books.

At this point, according to her English master, Steve Eddy, she did not stand out from her contemporaries. He said, she was 'one of a group of girls who were bright, and quite good at English'.

Even so, when she took A-levels in English, French and German she got two As and a B. She also became head girl. She tried to get into Oxford University but failed, going instead to Exeter University to read French and Classics. Here again, her main teacher, Martin Sorrell, remembers her only as 'a quietly competent student with a denim jacket and dark hair, who, in academic terms, gave the appearance of doing what was necessary'.

Rowling herself admitted that she did not work very hard. She graduated from Exeter in 1986 following a year in Paris and began working in London as a researcher and bilingual secretary at Amnesty International. In 1988 she began her writing career with a short essay about her time studying Classics. It was called *What was the Name of that Nymph Again? Or Greek and Roman Studies Recalled.* It was published by *Pegasus*, the journal of the University of Exeter.

When Rowling saw an advertisement in the *Guardian* inviting applicants to teach English she moved to Porto in Portugal. After eighteen months she met Jorge Arantes, a journalist. It turned out that they shared an interest in Jane Austen. They married in October 1992, soon had a daughter and named her Jessica (after Jessica Mitford). Unfortunately, the marriage did not work out and they separated in November 1993. Rowling left Portugal and moved with her daughter to Edinburgh to be near her sister.

It was a very low point for Rowling. She saw herself as a failure and even contemplated suicide! She signed up for welfare benefits describing her economic status as 'poor as it is possible to be in modern Britain, without being homeless'.

Rowling divorced Arantes in August 1994 and, while training to be a teacher, wrote her first novel in many

Edinburgh cafés including Nicolson's Café which was owned by her brother-in-law, Roger Moore.

In 1995 Rowling completed her first Harry Potter book, *Harry Potter and the Philosopher's Stone*. It had been typed on a manual typewriter. She signed up with Christopher Little literary agency to try and find a publisher. The agency approached twelve publishers all of whom turned it down. However, Nigel Newton, the Chairman of Bloomsbury, had given his eight-year-old daughter, Alice, a first chapter to read and, seeing her enthusiasm and demand for more chapters, Bloomsbury offered her a contract and paid her a £1,500 advance. Nevertheless, the editor, Barry Cunningham, advised her to get a day job as it was unlikely she could make a living by writing children's books.

Bloomsbury published *Philosopher's Stone* in 1997 with an initial print run of 1,000 copies, 500 of which went to libraries. Within five months the book won its first award and, in February 1998, it won the British Book Award for Children's Book of the Year. An auction for the right to publish the book in the USA was held in 1998 and was secured by Scholastic Inc. who paid $105,000. Rowling would say later that she 'nearly died' when she heard the news.

Other Harry Potter books soon followed – *Harry Potter and the Chamber of Secrets* in July 1998, *Harry Potter and the Prisoner of Azkaban* in December 1999, *Harry Potter and the Goblet of Fire* in July 2000. By this time sales were breaking records. No fewer than 372,775 copies of *Goblet of Fire* were sold on the first day in the UK! In the 2000 British Book Awards Rowling was named Author of the Year.

Next came *Harry Potter and the Order of the Phoenix* and the sixth novel, *Harry Potter and the Half-Blood Prince,* sold a staggering 9 million copies within 24 hours of its release. The seventh book, *Harry Potter and the Deathly Hallows*, beat even that, selling 11 million copies in the first 24 hours.

The enormously successful series of films of the novels followed.

All this turned Rowling into one of the richest people in the world. Indeed Forbes named her as the first person to become a US billionaire by writing books and said she was the 1,062nd richest person in the world. In its 2015 *Rich List* the *Sunday Times* placed her at the 193rd richest person in the UK, worth £580 million.

However, wealth is not necessarily influential. How has Rowling exerted influence?

She has made a huge contribution to popularising reading among children because her books are exciting and full of suspense. Children could not wait for the next release and to discuss them with their friends, and their popularity shows no sign of diminishing. They have been translated into 73 languages to date.

16. QUEEN ELIZABETH II

Queen Elizabeth came to the throne when her father, King George VI, died on 6 February 1952. He had reigned for only just over fifteen years after his older brother, about to be crowned King Edward VIII in 1937, had abdicated because the country's prevailing opinion 'disapproved' of his marriage to the divorced American Wallis Simpson.

Great Britain and its Empire were in a state of flux. Continuity of a stable monarchy was and remained the Queen's top priority. At least the Prime Minister, Winston

Churchill, tried to put her at her ease by saying in the House of Commons:

> A fair and youthful figure, Princess, wife and mother, is the heir to all our traditions and glories ... She comes to the throne at a time when a tormented mankind stands uncertainly poised between world catastrophe and a golden age. That it should be a golden age of art and letters we can only hope – science and machinery have their other tales to tell – but it is certain that if a true and lasting peace can be achieved ... an immense and undreamed of prosperity, with culture and leisure ever more widely spread, can come ... to the masses of the people.

In her reign there was an early example of the country's conservatism when permission was withheld for the Queen's younger sister, Margaret, to marry Group Captain Peter Townsend. The problem was he was divorced and the Church of England in particular was totally hostile.

Nevertheless, change was in the air. For example, Prince Charles, born in 1948, studied under a governess for only a short time before going to schools with other boys. The Queen had been educated privately at home. She spent her childhood as any aristocratic girl did in the 1930s in a world of dogs and horses rather than textbooks and schools. Her mother said:

> It is important to spend as long as possible in the open air, to enjoy to the full the pleasures of the country, to be able to dance and draw and appreciate music, to acquire good manners and perfect deportment, and to cultivate all the distinctive feminine graces.

The swinging 1960s brought many more changes, some of which, such as awarding MBEs to the Beatles, shocked the more conservative members of society. At the end of the 1960s a television programme, *Royal Family*, was broadcast showing the Queen, her husband Prince Philip and their four children enjoying everyday family life at both Windsor and Balmoral.

As a result of increased media attention public scrutiny encroached on Royal family life more and more, especially when Prince Charles married Lady Diana Spencer in 1981. National disapproval increased when, by 1992, three of the four marriages of the Queen's children had broken up. That year, which the Queen described as her *annus horribilis*, was not improved by a damaging fire at Windsor Castle, one of her favourite homes.

Worse was to follow in 1997 when Princess Diana, by this time divorced from Charles, was tragically killed at the young age of 36 in a motoring accident in Paris. To many of the public, the reaction of the Royal Family was too muted. For example the flag on Buckingham Palace was not lowered to half-mast. In response to this reaction, on the eve of Diana's funeral the Queen appeared on television to express her feelings of sorrow and regret in one of only two special addresses she has given in her entire reign. It was interesting that this speech had the desired effect and the Royal Family began to regain the country's love and respect.

The Queen has been influential in preserving the monarchy largely thanks to her persistence in preserving the dignity of and respect for the monarchy by resisting pressure to express personal opinions about her Governments' actions, be they Conservative (1952–1964, 1970–1974, 1979–1997 and 2010–2015) or Labour (1964–1970, 1974–1979 and 1997–2010).

Her influence is felt throughout the country through her patronage of over 600 organisations and charities. Her religious belief is strongly Christian and she is Supreme Governor of the Established Church of England. Although a Protestant herself, she has often demonstrated her support for inter-faith relations and has had meetings with the leaders of other churches and religions including five popes – Pius XII, John XXIII, John Paul II, Benedict XVI and Francis.

Her favourite quotation is said to be, 'Moderation in all things.'

Those who know her intimately say that behind her calm exterior there is a wry sense of humour as well as a capability to show flashes of temper. She has always been closely supported by her husband, Prince Philip, though he has been, at times, impatient with the emphasis on ritual and tradition and his lack of status and responsibility.

There have been critics of the Royal Family and the Queen, most notably, in the mid-1950s, Lord Altrincham and Malcolm Muggeridge, but they had relatively little impact. The Queen was persuaded to change her Christmas broadcast from radio to television. Although rather stilted for the first few years she gradually relaxed and it became a must for many families to watch it each Christmas Day.

Another of the Queen's great achievements is her support for the Commonwealth. There are 53 member countries in the Commonwealth ranging from the large, such as, the UK itself, India, Pakistan, Canada and Australia, through the many countries of Africa that were part of the former British Empire to the very small countries with populations of fewer than 2 million. All members subscribe to the Commonwealth's values and principles outlined in *The Commonwealth Charter* with its emphasis on democracy, human rights and the rule of law.

In summary, Queen Elizabeth has put the monarchy back to a level of popularity and significance not known since Queen Victoria's day. As Alan Titchmarsh put it, 'Hers has been a life of great privilege, undeniably, but more importantly it has been one of duty and service – two words which, for most of us now, seem at best quaint and at worst old fashioned – along with their dictionary companions loyalty, discretion, modesty and respect.'

15. TONY BLAIR

At 43 the youngest Prime Minister since Lord Liverpool in 1812, Tony Blair transformed the Labour Party after he became leader in 1994.

A few months after becoming leader he removed Clause IV from the Party's constitution. This meant the deletion of the party's commitment to 'the common ownership of the means of production and exchange' interpreted as wholesale nationalisation. At a conference in April 1995 the clause was replaced by a statement that the party is 'democratic socialist'.

At the Labour Party Conference the following year Blair said that his three priorities were 'education, education and education'.

By the time of the General Election in 1997 Blair's changes meant that the party was referred to as 'New Labour' and it easily overwhelmed John Major's tired Conservative Party, securing a majority of 179. In spite of Blair's commitment to modernisation and renewal Blair had told the voters, 'I am a modern man. I am part of the rock 'n' roll generation – the Beatles, colour TV, that's the generation I come from.'

And the Labour manifesto stated, 'We aim to put behind

us the bitter political struggles of left and right that have torn the country apart for too many decades. Many of these conflicts have no relevance whatsoever to the modern world – public versus private, bosses versus workers, middle class versus working class.'

Blair told voters in March 1997, 'People have to know that we will run from the centre and govern from the centre.'

Blair was educated at The Chorister School in Durham from the age of eight to thirteen and then at Fettes College, Edinburgh, a prestigious private boys' boarding school. This was unusual for a Labour leader, but not unique as Attlee had also been privately educated at Haileybury. Apparently, most of his masters were not very impressed and his biographer, John Rentoul, wrote, 'All the teachers I spoke to when researching the book said he was a complete pain in the backside and they were very glad to see the back of him.'

Blair went from Fettes to St John's College, Oxford where he was influenced by a fellow student, Peter Thomson, who was also an Anglican priest. Thomson deepened Blair's interest in religious faith and left-wing politics. After gaining a Second-Class Honours degree in Jurisprudence he became a member of Lincoln's Inn where he met his future wife, Cherie Booth.

His first two spells as Prime Minister seemed to be dominated by war. First he was faced in 1999 with a crisis in Kosovo where Slobodan Milosevic was indulging in wholesale slaughter. Blair sent in British troops and persuaded President Bill Clinton to send American forces too. When George W. Bush became President Blair joined him in sending troops, first, into Afghanistan in 2001 and second, into Iraq in 2003.

Nevertheless, Blair did enact measurements that were part of his modernisation programme. The first important and influential act was to give the Bank of England power to determine interest rates. This emphasised to business people and the City his support for commerce and industry.

This was soon followed by the Good Friday Agreement in Belfast in 1998 when Blair negotiated a settlement between Sinn Fein, on behalf of the IRA, and the mainstream parties. More negotiations were necessary but nevertheless this was a great achievement after years, decades even, of violence in Northern Ireland.

Another fine achievement – after centuries, never mind decades, of bigotry and prejudice – was the introduction of civil partnership for same sex couples.

Blair's constructive achievements as Prime Minister were:

The introduction of a National Minimum Wage

The enactment of some new employment rights (though Margaret Thatcher's anti-trade union legislation was retained)

The establishment of treaties integrating Britain more closely with the European Union

The introduction of market-based reforms in health and education

The introduction of student tuition fees

The ratification of tight anti-terrorism laws and identity card legislation

The enhancement of police powers by increasing the number of arrestable offences, and by introducing compulsory DNA recording and the use of dispersal orders.

New Labour also introduced devolution for Scotland and Wales, and brought in the European Declaration of Human Rights and the Freedom of Information Act.

Blair made the Labour Party attractive not only to the working class but to many in the middle class too. Some described his time in office as nothing more than 'Thatcherism with a human face'. Many would say there was nothing wrong with that.

If Margaret Thatcher was influential so was Tony Blair and he has admitted that during his term of office he learned the need to act fast and the importance of a determination to stay the course.

14. SIR ALEXANDER FLEMING

Alexander, later Sir Alexander, Fleming was the discoverer of penicillin which has saved, and continues to save, millions of lives.

This is what Fleming himself had to say about his discovery in the Nobel Lecture on 11 December 1945:

I am going to tell you about the early days of penicillin for this is the part of the penicillin story which earned me a Nobel Award [he was awarded it jointly with Sir Howard Florey and Sir Ernst Chain who carried on the development of the drug after Fleming's discovery] ... to tell the truth penicillin started as a chance observation. My only merit is that I did not neglect the observation and that I pursued the subject as a bacteriologist. My publication in 1929 was the starting-point of the work of others who developed penicillin especially in the chemical field ... In 1929, I published the results which I have briefly given to you and suggested that it would be useful for the treatment of infections with sensitive microbes. I referred again to penicillin in one or two publications up to 1936 but few people paid any attention. It was only when some 10 years later after the introduction of *sulphonamide* had completely changed the medical mind in regard to chemotherapy of bacterial infections, and after Dubos had shown that a powerful antibacterial agent, *gramicidin*, was produced by certain bacteria that my co-participators in this Nobel Award, Dr Chain and Sir Howard Florey, took up the investigation. They obtained my strain of *Penicillium notatum* and succeeded in concentrating penicillin with the result that now we have concentrated penicillin which is active beyond the wildest dreams I could possibly have had in those early days.

Almost incredibly, because Fleming was not a good communicator, his discovery was not given much attention. He presented a paper called *A Medium for the Isolation of Pfeiffer's Bacillus* to the medical research club of London in February 1929 but it did not arouse much interest or enthusiasm among its listeners or readers.

Nevertheless, Fleming conducted several experiments and the most significant result was proof that penicillin was non-toxic in human beings. By the end of the 1930s, Howard Florey, Ernst Chain, Norman Heatley and others were able to show that penicillin effectively cured bacterial infection in mice and, in 1941, they treated a policeman with a severe facial infection and carried on treating other people successfully. In 1941 Florey went to the USA to talk to pharmaceutical companies about mass production.

Gradually, production did increase and, in July 1943, The War Production Board drew up a plan to supply all the Allied troops fighting in Europe (Italy in 1943 and also France and Germany in 1944/5). In all, 2.3 million doses had been produced by the time the Allies invaded Normandy in June

1944. By June 1945, no fewer than 646 billion units a year were being produced.

Fleming was modest about his part in the 'development' of penicillin and described his fame as the 'Fleming Myth'. He always gave the credit to Florey and Chain. Nevertheless, as Sir Henry Harris, a scientist at Oxford, famous for his work on cancer, said in 1988, 'Without Fleming no Chain; without Chain no Florey; without Florey, no Heatley; without Heatley, no penicillin.'

Fleming made many speeches throughout the world and significantly he always gave warnings about the use of penicillin, noting particularly that bacteria developed antibiotic resistance if penicillin was used for too short a period or in too small quantities.

There were many memorials to Fleming after his death in 1955 and, as Kevin Brown said in his biography of Fleming – *Penicillin Man* – 'People have never forgotten Fleming's name in the wider world. When the approach of a new millennium concentrated minds on the achievements of the old, it was inevitable that the discovery of penicillin should be seen as one of the defining moments of the twentieth century ... Readers of the *Scotsman* voted for Fleming as the Scot of the century ... *The Times* voted for penicillin as a national millennium treasure in 2000.'

Fleming's discovery led to an expansion in the pharmaceutical industry and by the end of the Second World War, penicillin would be curing some of the diseases that had afflicted mankind for centuries such as syphilis, gangrene and tuberculosis.

13. THE BEATLES

The Beatles, with their two dominant performers John Lennon and Paul, now Sir Paul, McCartney, dominated pop music in the 1960s, not only in Britain but throughout the world even including the USA. The coined word 'Beatlemania' was used by the media to describe their huge following. Until they burst on to the international music scene, British groups had tended to be seen as poor relations to such American stars as Bill Haley, Elvis Presley and Buddy Holly.

The Beatles group was founded in 1956 when Lennon got together with McCartney. George Harrison joined in 1957 to be followed by Pete Best, as drummer, in 1960, who was replaced two years later by Ringo Starr. The group was founded as the Quarrymen but in the four years from 1956 to 1960 it played under several names – Johnny & the Moondogs, Silver Beatles and finally the Beatles. In those early days, like other groups, the Beatles played in coffee bars and small teenage clubs and for very little money.

The upward move began when they played at a nightclub in Hamburg's notorious Reeperbahn in 1960 and various other nightclubs in Hamburg over the following two years. One of the songs they recorded there came to the notice of Brian Epstein who was running the record department in his family's store in Liverpool. When Epstein met them he was impressed and said later, 'I immediately liked what I heard. They were fresh and they were honest, and they had what I thought was a sort of presence … a star quality.'

He started to act for them as their manager but initially he was turned down by every major recording company in Britain. However, he persisted and, in 1962, secured a recording contract with the EMI subsidiary Parlophone.

Their first hit was *Love Me Do*, recorded in the autumn of 1962. They soon acquired the nickname 'the Fab Four' as Beatlemania grew. By 1964 they had become international stars. On 7 February they flew from London's Heathrow airport, where 4,000 fans waved and screamed as the aircraft took off, to New York's Kennedy Airport, where again there were about 3,000 expectant fans waiting to greet them noisily.

Two days later they gave their first live television performance on *The Ed Sullivan Show* and were watched by 73 million viewers in over 23 million households. The Nielsen rating service said it was the largest audience ever for an American television programme.

Further visits to the USA took place and in 1965 Elvis Presley, an early influence on them, invited them to his home in Beverly Hills. Lennon had said of Presley, 'Nothing really affected me till I heard Elvis. If there hadn't been Elvis, there would not have been the Beatles.'

On 25 June 1967 the Beatles performed their forthcoming single, *All You Need Is Love*, to an estimated 300 million viewers on *Our World*, the first live global television link.

While all this excitement was going on Her Majesty Queen Elizabeth appointed Lennon, McCartney, Harrison and Starr Members of the British Empire – this delighted some and appalled others.

In 1966 the Beatles recorded *Sgt. Pepper's Lonely Hearts Club Band*, the recording of which took over 700 hours. According to engineer Geoff Emerick:

> Everything had to be different. We had microphones right down in the bells of brass instruments and headphones turned into microphones attached to violins. We used giant

oscillators to vary the speed of instruments and vocals and we had tapes chopped to pieces and stuck together upside down and the wrong way round.

Author Jonathan Gould wrote:

The overwhelming consensus is that the Beatles had created a popular masterpiece: a rich, sustained, and overflowing work of collaborative genius whose bold ambition and startling originality dramatically enlarged the possibilities and raised the expectations of what the experience of listening to popular music on record could be. On the basis of this perception, *Sgt. Pepper* became the catalyst for an explosion of mass enthusiasm for album-formatted rock that would revolutionise both the aesthetics and the economics of the record business in ways that far outstripped the earlier pop explosions triggered by the Elvis phenomenon of 1956 and the Beatlemania phenomenon of 1963.

As well as their MBEs, the Beatles received many other awards, accolades and achievements: the film *Let It Be* (1970) won the 1971 Academy Award for Best Original Song Score. The recipients of 10 Grammy Awards, an Academy Award for best Original Song Score and 15 Ivor Novello Awards, the group have been awarded 6 Diamond Albums, as well as 24 Multi-Platinum albums, 39 Platinum albums and 45 Gold albums in the United States. In the UK, the Beatles have four Multi-Platinum albums, four Platinum albums, eight Gold albums and one Silver album. They were inducted as a group into the Rock and Roll Hall of Fame in 1988, as well as each being individually inducted between 1994 and 2015.

Collectively included in *Time* magazine's compilation of the 100 Most Important People of the 20th Century pub-

lished in 1999, the Beatles are the best-selling band in history, having sold between 600 million and (at EMI estimates) over a billion units worldwide. They have had more number-one albums on the British charts (15), and sold more singles in the UK (21.9 million), than any other act. According to the Recording Industry Association of America, the Beatles are the best-selling music artists in the United States, with 178 million certified units, more than any other artist. In 2004, *Rolling Stone* magazine ranked the Beatles as the Best Artist of All Time, and in 2008 on *Billboard* magazine's list of the all-time most successful Hot 100 artists, released in 2008 to celebrate the US singles chart's 50th anniversary, they ranked number one. As of 2015 they hold the record for the most number-one hits on the *Billboard* Hot 100, with 20.

The Beatles unquestionably dominated the pop music of the 1960s and, as we have seen, led their own group as well as other British groups, such as The Rolling Stones, to the top of the world pop music scene. In 2014, they received the Grammy Lifetime Achievement Award.

12. SIR JONATHAN IVE

Jonathan, now Sir Jonathan, Ive, also known as Jony, became not only famous but hugely influential through his work at the fabulously successful company Apple. He collaborated closely with the Apple boss, Steve Jobs, starting with the iMac. They were both driven to find a better way.

As Leander Kahney wrote in his biography, *Jony Ive: The Genius Behind Apple's Greatest Products*:

The products that followed sent Jony deep into new materials and manufacturing methods, driven by his desire always to find a better way. The iPod was a product of Jony's simplification philosophy. It could have been just another complex MP3 player, but instead he turned it into the iconic gadget that set the design cues for later mobile devices. Two more delightful innovations, the iPhone and iPad, were products of thinking differently, of creative engineering at work in rational problem solving on many levels.

Andrew Hargadon, a design and innovation professor at the University of California, said:

When the iMac first came out in jelly bean colours, so many other different products came out following that lead. There were staplers in six jelly bean colors. The iMac turned consumers into design aficionados to a much greater degree than they were before.

Hargadon also said:

'That's probably the single greatest effect, that we nowadays expect many things to have better designs. Because of Apple, we got to compare crappy portable computers versus really nice ones, crappy phones versus really nice ones. We saw a before-and-after effect. Not over a generation, but within a few years. Suddenly 600 million people had a phone that put to shame the phone they used to have. That is a design education at work within our culture.

Jonathan Ive was born in Chingford, London on 27 February 1967. He was educated at Chingford Foundation School and Walton High School before going to Newcastle Polytechnic, now Northumbria University, to study industrial design.

Some of his items, such as a hearing aid design, were exhibited at the Design Museum in London. His first job was at the London design agency Roberts Weaver Group, which had sponsored him at college.

After a year at Roberts Weaver he moved to a new design agency, Tangerine in Hoxton Square, and designed various different products including a microwave oven and toothbrushes. One of Tangerine's clients was Apple and Ive moved there in 1992. Apple had been going through some difficult times but, when Steve Jobs, its original boss, moved back in 1997, Ive was appointed Senior Vice President of Industrial Design. His first design assignment was the iMac and this was followed by many other designs including the iPod, the iPhone and the iPad.

Later in 2012 Jony was promoted to become Apple's overall creative boss. The new chief executive, Tim Cook, said:

Jony has an incredible design aesthetic and has been the driving force behind the look and feel of our products for more than a decade. The face of many of our products is our software and the extension of Jony's skills into this area will widen the gap between Apple and our competition … Jony is one of the most talented and accomplished designers of his generation with an astonishing 5,000 design and utility patents to his name.

Jobs had always had great faith in Jony and said of him:

He understands business concepts, marketing concepts. He picks stuff up just like that, click … He understands what we do at our core better than anyone. If I had a spiritual partner at Apple, it's Jony. Jony and I think up most of the products together and then pull others in and say, 'Hey, what do you think about this?' He gets the big picture as well as the most infinitesimal details about each product. And he understands that Apple is a product company. He's not just a designer.

He later confirmed, 'Jony has more operational power than anyone else at Apple except me.'

And Clive Grinyer, Jony's first business partner, said:

Jony never was just the designer. He always played a much more strategic role at Apple. That includes also the user interface for which he also helped make the decisions ... Jony is now in the strategic position. I always felt very optimistic about Apple, because so much of Apple's success has been due to Jony. Steve unlocked Jony. Steve took Jony away from printer lids and gave him the job he was capable of ... Steve gave Jony the confidence to bring out his innate design talent and create amazing products. And from now he will carry on as normal. Apple was already a pretty amazing company, but the level they have reached in the last ten years is because they have had Jony, empowered by Steve, to produce that incredible panel of work.

Just after Steve Job's death on 5 October 2011, Apple launched the iPhone 4s. It was Jony Ive's third generation design and was the most advanced iPhone up to that date. Some felt it was overhyped but the general public loved it and no fewer than 4 million units were sold the first weekend after its launch.

Wall Street noticed and Apple's stock began to soar. A share of Apple's stock sold for $407.61 on 3 January 2012, reflecting a balance sheet that contained over $100 billion in cash, a sum that grew by the day. By the end of January, a single share of Apple cost $447.61.

Apple rode past Exxon Mobile to become the most valuable publicly held company in the world.

Jony Ive's achievements were recognised in the 2012 New Year Honours List when he was made a Knight Commander of the British Empire and became Sir Jonathan Ive (he had already been made a CBE in 2005). He told the *Daily Telegraph* that he was 'the product of a very British design education', adding that 'even in high school, I was keenly aware of this remarkable tradition that the UK had of designing and making. It's important to remember that Britain was the first country to industrialise, so I think there's a strong argument to say that this is where my profession was founded.'

11. ROY JENKINS

Roy Jenkins is the most influential politician of the last 100 years who was never Prime Minister.

Born into a working-class Welsh family (his father worked down the coalmines before entering politics and becoming an aid to Clement Attlee) Jenkins was nevertheless most at home among the upper classes in London.

He was born in 1920 and after school in South Wales he went to the scholarly Balliol College at Oxford University where Edward Heath and Denis Healey were undergraduates in the same college. He mixed with them and plenty of other intellectual and angry future politicians.

During the Second World War he spent some time at the code-breaking centre Bletchley Park and, after the War, went into politics. In the 1950s he became friendly with the Labour Party leader, Hugh Gaitskell, and settled on the social-democratic, rather than left-wing side of the Labour Party.

In 1964, at the age of 43, Jenkins was appointed Minister of Aviation in Harold Wilson's Labour Government when it won the General Election of 1964. He immediately proved himself effective and was promoted to Home Secretary in 1965. His biographer wrote of his achievements in the following two years, 'He ended flogging in prisons; secured Government time to ensure the passage of Private Members' bills on both homosexuality and abortion.'

Jenkins had written in 1959, 'The law relating to homo-sexuality remains in the brutal and unfair state in which the House of Commons almost accidentally placed it in 1885.'

On the more conventional marriage front, Jenkins was also responsible for relaxing the strict laws governing divorce.

He wrote in his autobiography, 'The divorce laws which involve both a great deal of unnecessary suffering and a great number of attempts (many of them successful) to deceive the courts were in urgent need of reform.'

Of abortion, he wrote, 'The harsh and archaic abortion laws were also indefensible.'

Jenkins initiated the ending of theatre censorship and introduced a ground-breaking Race Relations bill.

The Race Relations Act 1965 outlawed direct discrimin-ation on the grounds of race, colour, and ethnic or national origin in some public places. The legislation also set up a Race Relations Board. A centrally financed network of local officers was provided to smooth inter-racial relations by conciliation, education and informal pressure, while a National Committee for Commonwealth Immigrants was established (under the chairmanship of the Archbishop of Canterbury) to encourage and help finance staff 'for local

voluntary, good-neighbour type bodies'. A further Race Relations Act 1968 was passed, which made discrimination in letting or advertising housing illegal, together with discrimination in hiring and promotion. The legislation also provided a strengthened Race Relations Board with powers to 'conciliate' in cases of discrimination, which meant taking measures to persuade discriminators to cease such acts and, if they refused, legal action could be taken against them as an ultimate sanction. The legislation also replaced the National Committee for Commonwealth Immigrants with the Community Relations Commission, a statutory body. This body was provided with an annual grant beginning at £300,000 (£6 million today) for social work, propaganda and education as a means of bringing about good race relations. The Criminal Justice Act 1967 introduced suspended prison sentences and allowed a ten to two majority vote for jury decisions. An Ombudsman (Parliamentary Commissioner) was appointed in 1967 to consider complaints against Government departments and to impose remedies, while censorship of plays by the Lord Chamberlain was abolished (1969). In addition, the law on Sunday Observance was relaxed, and an enhancement of legal aid provision was implemented.

Immigration was a divisive and provocative issue during the late 1960s and on 23 May 1966 Jenkins delivered a speech on race relations, which is widely considered to be one of his best. Addressing a London meeting of the National Committee for Commonwealth Immigrants he notably defined Integration ' … not as a flattening process of assimilation but as equal opportunity, accompanied by cultural diversity, in an atmosphere of mutual tolerance' before going on to ask: 'Where in the world is there a university which could preserve its fame, or a cultural centre which could keep its eminence, or a metropolis which could hold its drawing power, if it were to turn inwards and serve only its own hinterland and its own racial group?'

And concluding that: 'To live apart, for a person, a city, a country, is to lead a life of declining intellectual stimulation.'

Capital punishment was also abolished in 1965.

In short, perhaps more than any other politician of the 20th century, Jenkins shaped the society Britons inhabit in the early 21st century.

When he was criticised for helping to create a 'a permissive society' he said, 'The permissive society has been allowed to become a dirty phrase. A better phrase is the civilized society'.

After his success as Home Secretary he succeeded James Callaghan as Chancellor of the Exchequer when Callaghan resigned following what was generally seen as the humiliating devaluation of the pound sterling in November 1967. As Chancellor he felt his job was to steady the ship and he introduced what was seen as a tough Budget in 1968 increasing taxes by £923 million (nearly £25 billion today taking a billion as 1,000 million). It was more than twice the increase made in any previous budget.

He increased taxation further in late 1968 and in the Budget of 1969 but by May 1969 Britain's current account was in surplus. His time as Chancellor of the Exchequer has received praise from both economists and historians. For example, Andrew Marr said he had been one of the century's 'most successful chancellors'.

10. MARIE STOPES

Although Marie Stopes was an author, poet, palaeobotanist, eugenicist and campaigner for women's rights, her influence comes from her pioneering work in the field of birth control.

Born in 1880 to an archaeologist father and a mother who was a suffragist, she went to universities in London, Munich and Manchester where she became the first female member of the science faculty.

During the First World War she wrote a book about feminism and marriage. The book was called *Married Love* and in it she argued that marriage should be an equal relationship between husband and wife. She had great difficulty finding a publisher. Walter Blackie of the publishers Blackie & Son said, 'The theme does not please me. I think there is far too much talking and writing about these matters already.'

He also objected to this assertion in the book, 'far too often, marriage puts an end to women's intellectual life. Marriage can never reach its full stature until women possess as much intellectual freedom of opportunity within it as do their partners.'

However, Marie Stopes did eventually find a publisher willing to publish her book and, when it was published in March 1918, it was an immediate success and had to be reprinted five times.

She followed *Married Love* with *Wise Parenthood* which was a guide to contraception. The Church of England, and more especially Roman Catholics, reacted strongly against the book and the Pope made it clear that he was against all forms of contraception.

In spite of this, in 1921 Stopes founded The Society for Constructive Birth Control and Racial Progress. With financial help from her second husband, Humphrey Roe (her first marriage had been dissolved after three years without consummation), she opened the first of her birth-control clinics in Holloway, north London on 17 March 1921. This was a brave thing to do as a number of people had been sent to prison for advocating birth control. Indeed, Halliday Sutherland wrote an article in the *Daily Express* calling for her to be sent to prison and wrote a book in which he attacked her publications as obscene.

Meanwhile the clinic, run by midwives and supported by visiting doctors, was giving mothers birth control advice and teaching them birth control methods. The clinic was free and was open to all married women.

Stopes did not like abortion and tried to find alternatives such as the cervical cap, *coitus interruptus*, and spermicides based on oil and soap. She re-introduced the use of olive oil-soaked sponges.

In 1925 the Mother's Clinic moved from Holloway to Central London and is still operating in 2015. She also built up a small network of clinics, Leeds in 1934, Aberdeen also in 1934, Belfast in 1936, Cardiff in 1937 and Swansea in 1943.

Other birth-control clinics gradually spread throughout Britain beginning with one in Wolverhampton in 1926. Two horse-drawn caravans, converted into mobile clinics, toured the country bringing advice and instruction to women in Wales and the North of England. There was still considerable opposition but advocates of birth control worked on local authorities to open clinics. By 1939 there were nearly 100, and Stopes's National Birth Control Association had become the Family Planning Association.

By the late 1930s birth rates were falling sharply and by

1940, only 9 per cent of women had families of more than five children and only 30 per cent three or more. As Juliet Gardiner put it in her book *The Thirties*, 'the post-First World War middle-class norm of the two child family was beginning to permeate to the working classes'.

The clinics continued after Stopes's death in 1958 but in the 1970s faced financial difficulties and went into voluntary receivership. However Marie Stopes International was then founded as an international non-governmental organisation. It has grown so it now operates with 452 clinics in over 40 countries.

Marie Stopes International says that it 'exists to bring quality family planning and reproductive healthcare to the world's poorest and most vulnerable people. We've been delivering family planning, safe abortion, and material health services for over 35 years.'

It promotes itself under the headings:

Commitment to saving lives
Giving people a choice
Working in under-served communities
Working in partnership

9. ROBERT BADEN-POWELL

Robert, later Baron, Baden-Powell founded and built up the Boy Scout movement.

Tim Jeal wrote in his biography of Baden-Powell,

Since its inception in 1908, Baden-Powell's Movement has attracted approximately 500 million members (4 million of

whom are currently Scouts in America). With the exception of great religions and political ideologies, no international organisation has exerted a greater influence upon social behaviour than the Boy and Girl Guides.

In July 1906 Baden-Powell had spent a fortnight with Arthur Pearson, owner of the *Daily Express* and the *Evening Standard,* at his house in Frensham, Surrey and as Tim Jeal recorded in his biography:

Two weeks after staying with Pearson, Baden-Powell was writing about his plans to 'draw up a scheme with a handbook to it for the education of Boys as Scouts'. This is the first mention of the 'handbook', which would become not only one of the world's greatest best sellers but the Boy Scouts Bible: on one level a 'how to do it' manual, but on another an almost theological statement of purposes and principles. Baden-Powell's weekend in the Surrey countryside brought him appreciably closer to launching the Boy Scouts. But it would still take him a year and a half of hard work and many meetings with his assiduous backer to bring his 'handbook' to press.

By November 1907 Baden-Powell was ready to talk about his Boy Scouts' scheme and from that month to February 1908 he gave over 50 lectures.

In January 1908 Part One of *Scouting for Boys* was distributed to bookstalls. In it Baden-Powell told scouting instructors, 'Instruction in Scouting should be given as far as possible in practices, games and competitions. Games should be organised mainly as team matches, when the patrol forms a team, and every boy is playing, not merely looking on.'

This was the Scout Law proposed by Baden-Powell:

The Scout motto is:

BE PREPARED

Which means you are always to be in a state of mind and body to do your DUTY

The Scout law

1. A SCOUT'S HONOUR IS TO BE TRUSTED
If a Scout says 'On my honour it is so,' that means that it is so, just as if he had taken a most solemn oath …

2. A SCOUT IS LOYAL to the King, and to his officers, and to his parents, his country, and his employers. He must stick to them through thick and thin against anyone who is their enemy or who even talks badly of them.

3. A SCOUT'S DUTY IS TO BE USEFUL AND TO HELP OTHERS.
And he is to do his duty before anything else, even though he gives up his own pleasure, or comfort, or safety to do it. When in difficulty to know which of two things to do, he must ask himself, 'Which is my duty?' that is, 'Which is for other people?' – and do that one. He must Be Prepared at any time to save life, or to help injured persons. And he must try his best to do a good turn to somebody every day.

4. A SCOUT IS A FRIEND TO ALL, AND A BROTHER TO EVERY OTHER SCOUT, NO MATTER TO WHAT SOCIAL CLASS THE OTHER BELONGS.
Thus if a scout meets another scout, even though a stranger to him, he must speak to him, and help him in any way that he

can ... A Scout must never be a SNOB. A snob is one who looks down upon another because he is poorer, or who is poor and resents another because he is rich. A Scout accepts the other man as he finds him, and makes the best of him ...

5. A SCOUT IS COURTEOUS: That is, he is polite to all – but especially to women and children, and old people and invalids, cripples, etc. And he must not take any reward for being helpful or courteous.

6. A SCOUT IS A FRIEND TO ANIMALS. He should save them as far as possible from pain, and should not kill any animal unnecessarily, even if it is only a fly – for it is one of God's creatures. Killing an animal for food is allowable.

7. A SCOUT OBEYS ORDERS of his parents, patrol leader, or Scoutmaster without question. Even if he gets an order he does not like he must do as soldiers and sailors do, he must carry it out all the same because it is his duty; and after he has done it he can come and state any reasons against it: but he must carry out the order at once. That is discipline.

8. A SCOUT SMILES AND WHISTLES under all circumstances. When he gets an order he should obey it cheerily and readily, not in a slow, hang-dog sort of way. Scouts never grouse at hardships, nor whine at each other nor swear when put out ... You should force yourself to smile at once, and then whistle a tune, and you will be all right. A Scout goes about with a smile on and whistling. It cheers him and cheers other people, especially in time of danger ... The punishment for swearing or using bad language is for each offence a mug of cold water to be poured down the offender's sleeve by the other Scouts ...

9. A SCOUT IS THRIFTY, that is, he saves every penny he can.

The success of his book, *Scouting for Boys*, which was published in full later the same year and which is said to be the fourth most popular in the world (after the Bible, the Quran and Mao's Little Red Book) has been almost unequalled by that of any other. Originally published at 2/- (10p, or £10 today) in cloth and 1/- in paper it sold over 60,000 in its first year and continued to sell steadily for the next 50 years. In 1948, its 40th anniversary, it sold over 50,000 copies. Sales overseas were also impressive and by the late 1920s it was being printed in 26 countries. Overall, only the Bible has sold more copies in the 20th century.

What about girls? Could they be Scouts too?

Initially Baden-Powell did not like the idea but he came round to it and in 1907 in his first Boy Scouts' Scheme pamphlet described Scouting as the basis 'for an attractive organisation and valuable training for girls'.

He asked his sister, Agnes Baden-Powell, to form a Girl Guides' Committee and the number of Girl Guides grew rapidly from 1910 onwards. There are now millions of Guides throughout the world and internationally they are governed by the World Association of Girl Guides and Girl Scouts which has members in no fewer than 145 countries.

Baden-Powell's first experiment with a Scout camp took place in 1907, on Brownsea Island in Dorset, but it was in the 1920s that Scouting reached the zenith of its prestige. Its original mixture of patriotism, a whiff of the military and outdoor adventures for urban children made this a 'how shall we live?' movement shorn of sexual and political issues of adult back-to-the-landers. In those days, clusters of small ex-army tents full of working-class boys ruled over by wiry ex-military Scoutmasters could be found in woods across

Britain, a Union Jack hanging from a nearby tree. In city streets, small boys carrying whistles and sticks, dressed in the khaki shirt, shorts and floppy hats which Baden-Powell had copied from the South African police force, marched around looking for opportunities to carry out good deeds.

Scouting was a rare British cultural export. The imperialism and jingoism of the pre-War movement was replaced by a new emphasis on internationalism and brotherhood, and by 1922 there were 3 million Scouts in 32 countries. One early convert was a young Lake District artist called John Hargrave, who supplied the drawings for John Buchan's novels. Impoverished and a Quaker, Hargrave moved to London, where he became a newspaper cartoonist and writer on Scouting under the name White Fox. He rose fast through the Scouting movement and was seen as an obvious successor to Baden-Powell. But Hargrave, a pacifist, fell out with the military hero and in 1920 was expelled from the Scouts.

In 1919 Baden-Powell became President of the Camping Club of Great Britain and Ireland, which held its first Club Feast of Lanterns at Deep Dene in Dorking in 1921 – Chinese lanterns rather than Indian tents and Nordic headdresses, but yet a more bosky ritual.

The first international Scout Jamboree took place in 1920 and afterwards Baden-Powell was solemnly declared Chief Scout of the World. A year later he was created a baronet.

8. VLADIMIR RAITZ

Raitz was a classic example of the benefits Britain gained from the persecution of the Jews in Russia and Germany.

Born into a middle-class family in Moscow in 1922, his father sent the family first to Berlin and then to Vienna. Nazi persecution meant Vladimir Raitz arrived in London in 1936 without being able to speak a word of English. Nevertheless he went to the London School of Economics and worked as a news agency translator in the Second World War. It was when he was on holiday in 1949 in Calvi, Corsica that he came up with the idea of cut-price holidays.

He was the first businessman to offer charter flights and all-inclusive holidays. His first package was in May 1950 when all the passengers flew to Corsica on a Government-surplus Dakota DC3. The aircraft landed at Nice to refuel and the holiday makers slept in tents on arrival. In total they paid £32.50 (about £950 today) which was less than half the cost of a scheduled flight to Nice at the time, which was £70 (or about £2,000 today).

As well as the return flight and the tented accommodation on the beach, he offered 'delicious meat filled meals and as much local wine as could be put away'.

Raitz said later, 'When we arrived at Corsica airport, there was nothing at all – not even a little hut. We had to shelter from the sun under the wings of the plane while we waited for the bus to pick us up.'

On the beach the holidaymakers found large canvas tents, each with two beds. There was an area set aside for ablutions and there was a dining room, bar and dance floor.

Raitz remembered that 'A pastis was a few pence and a bottle of wine was nine pence' (4.5p or less than £1.50 today).

The company he had founded, with £3,000 (about £90,000 today) left him by his grandfather, was called Horizon Holidays. He met a great deal of opposition both from business rivals and, more bizarrely, from the Government. For example, initially he was given permission to offer his

holidays only to students and teachers. In spite of this, Horizon became one of the country's biggest tour operators. It soon added Majorca, Sardinia, Malaga and Perpignan (for access to the Costa Brava) to its destinations.

There were soon plenty of imitators and by 1960, 2.25 million Britons were taking holidays abroad. By 1967 it was 5 million. By 2015 it was over 20 million.

By 1970, Raitz could say this about Horizon Holidays:

Horizon now had its own travel agency outlet in Central London (in Maddox Street, off Regent Street), and was, over the years, to establish fifteen branches across the UK in towns like Nottingham, Cardiff, Bristol, Manchester and Glasgow. Our offices at 146 Fleet Street had become far too small, and we set up new headquarters in Hanover Street in the West End – an area that was rapidly becoming the location for many airline offices and National Tourist shops, and was becoming what Harley Street was to doctors and Bond Street was to high-class jewellers.

Further expansion of our tour operating programme was the number one priority. Let me briefly review the Horizon Holidays brochure of 1970. It consisted of 196 pages of text and colour photographs, compared to our four page black and white mimeographed leaflet of the years 1950 and 1951. The cover showed a reproduction of a painting by Raoul Duffy of a south of France seascape (very different from our competitors' brochure covers, showing couples or families lying on deckchairs on the beach), and was supposed to underline Horizon's sophistication and exclusivity.

All of our flights were now entirely by jet aircraft. We used the BAC 1-11s of British United Airways, which had absorbed Gerry Freeman's Transair, as well as British United's VC10s for our long-haul holidays, and some of BOAC's 707s, BEA's

Comets and Britannia's 737s. In addition to the traditional seaside holiday, Horizon was now offering holidays in villas, coach tours, Mediterranean cruises, and a 'Far Horizons' range of holidays to the Americas and the Far East. The brochure featured holidays to the south of France – Cannes, Menton and Nice – in Corsica, our old stalwart Calvi had been augmented by Algajola and Propriano. Long, exploratory car journeys by myself and colleagues throughout Italy had yielded many resorts on the Neapolitan Riviera such as Amalfi, Positano and Sorrento. The Venetian and Adriatic coasts were well represented, as were Sicily, Sardinia and other islands like Capri and Ischia. The Greek mainland and a multiplicity of her islands was well featured, and also Yugoslavia, which was making a powerful entrance on to the tourism market at that time. Portugal, Tunisia and Turkey were also featured, and the Soviet Union and the USA were included for the first time.

I had also created, in conjunction with two large travel agents (one in Birmingham and the other in Wolverhampton), a new tour operator, flying to the most popular Mediterranean resorts from Birmingham and East Midlands airports. This company was named Horizon Midlands and was, in 1972, to be floated as a public company – the first travel organization to do so.

An independently commissioned opinion poll had asked travel agents throughout the UK to rank all the major tour companies in order of preference on seven different counts:

Which company had the highest standard of accommodation?
Which company had the fewest complaints?
Which company had the most charter plane experience?
Which company had the best brochure?
Which company had the widest choice of resorts?

Which company would the agent recommend to his most
discerning clients?
Which company would the agent choose for his own holiday?

Horizon came out as first choice in all seven categories. No
wonder, then, that we featured this fact prominently in our
literature, and also used it in a TV commercial in which travel
agents appeared as cartoon characters, shouting 'Horizon!' as
each of the questions was put to them by an announcer.

In 1965 Raitz bought two of his rivals, Sky Tours and Riviera
Holidays, and, with a small carrier, Britannia Airways,
formed Thomson Holidays. In 1970 he founded Club 18–30.

The early 1970s proved to be tough with increasing
competition and a sharp escalation in the price of oil in
1973/4, and in 1974 Horizon was taken over by Court Line,
the owner of the biggest tour operator, Clarksons Travel
Group. Clarksons then collapsed, owing £7 million to no
fewer than 100,000 holidaymakers.

In spite of this crisis Raitz remained in the travel business,
becoming involved in the Association of British Travel
Agents (ABTA) and as a board member of Air Malta as well
as Managing Director of Medallion Holidays.

He would later say, 'The man in the street acquired a taste
for wine, for foreign food, started to learn French, Spanish
or Italian, made friends in the foreign lands he visited – in
fact, became more cosmopolitan … it's marvellous that 12 or
13 million people can have a Mediterranean holiday.'

A measurement of the growth of package holidays comes
from the fact that in 1952 a survey by the *Daily Herald* showed
that only 1.5 per cent of the British population took a holiday
abroad. By 1989 the number of packages was 14.2 million.

7. SIR ALLEN LANE

Allen Lane, born as Allen Lane Williams, on 21 September 1902, became a publisher and founded Penguin Books, a publisher of paperback books which enabled people to buy high quality fiction and non-fiction books at a much lower price than had been available earlier.

Born in Bristol to Camilla, née Lane, and Samuel Williams, he was educated at Bristol Grammar School and joined the publisher Bodley Head in 1919 at the age of sixteen, as an apprentice to John Lane, his uncle and the founder of Bodley Head. He and the rest of his family changed their surname to retain the childless John Lane's company as a family firm. He was paid a guinea (£1 and 1 shilling) a week (about £60 or £3,000 a year today). He had to pay nearly half this to board with his uncle.

By 1925 he was Managing Editor and a director after his uncle died but he left Bodley Head in 1936. He had fallen out with the directors after they had opposed publication of James Joyce's controversial book *Ulysses*. Lane and his brothers, Richard and John, had founded Penguin Books as part of Bodley Head in 1935 and it became a separate company in 1936.

Apparently, this idea of printing and publishing paperbacks came to Allen Lane when he was returning from Devon with his favourite Bodley Head author, Agatha Christie, and was irritated when he could not find a book he considered worth reading at the bookstall on Exeter Station. Sitting on the train from Exeter to London he passed the time by imagining the publication of high quality fiction and non-fiction books at the cost of sixpence (2.5p or about

£1.50 today). In those days this was the price of a packet of ten cigarettes.

He talked to his fellow directors at Bodley Head about the possibility (he had become Chairman in 1930 at the age of 28) but they did not like the idea. Paperbacks were looked on as 'dirty rubbish' by publishers. Paperbacks had been around for years as 'railway novels' or 'penny dreadfuls' in the UK and 'dime novels' in the USA. However, they were looked on as trash, not proper books. Nevertheless, they grudgingly agreed that Allen Lane could pursue his idea.

The logo of the waddling Penguin was drawn by an artist working for Bodley Head, Edward Young, who was sent to London Zoo for inspiration. The paperback idea was the start of a revolution but its success seemed to be in the balance until the retail chain F.W. Woolworth placed an order for 63,000 copies. Apparently the buyer did not like the books but his wife did. This led to Penguin Books being set up as a separate company. The starting capital was £1,000 (£60,000 today) and there were three directors, Lane and his brothers.

The Penguin books were cheap, though well printed and only a little larger than a 1930s cigarette packet. Lane decreed that the books would not have pictures and none of what he described as 'bosoms and bottoms' on the covers. The covers were to be green for crime stories, orange for other fiction and blue for non-fiction with the title in plain lettering on a white background. The design aimed at simple clarity. Lane deliberately mixed serious with popular writing and commissioned André Maurois and George Bernard Shaw but also Agatha Christie and Dorothy L. Sayers. During the Second World War, which broke out in 1939, copies of Penguin books were sent all over the world to wherever British forces were fighting.

Their popularity was helped by the formation of several book clubs.

Real growth came after the Second World War and by the 1960s paperbacks were booming. For example Mills & Boon switched from hardbacks to paperbacks at the beginning of the 1960s. By 1970 sales of paperbacks had reached about 90 million a year. This accounted for 40 per cent of total publishing income.

Penguin was still the market leader in paperbacks. In 1960 there were 6,000 Penguin paperbacks in print and by 1970 there were more than 37,000 which accounted for about a third of all paperback sales. The number of copies was 29 million. Pan was second with 20 million. Pan was fortunate to have the James Bond thrillers. Of the first eighteen books to sell a million copies, ten were James Bond titles.

Allen Lane was knighted in 1952 and died of cancer in 1970, aged only 67. His daughter married Michael Morpurgo, the very successful author of children's books, including *War Horse*. J.E. Morpurgo (no relation) wrote a biography, *Allen Lane: King Penguin*, and *inter alia*, said Lane had created 'an institution of national and international importance like *The Times* or the BBC'.

And *The Times* itself wrote a leader in 1950 which congratulated Allen Lane for helping make up for the loss of the British Empire by using his cheap paperbacks to spread British influence over millions of people throughout the world, something less objectionable but just as powerful as British imperialism.

6. EMMELINE PANKHURST

Born on 15 July 1858 in Moss Side, Manchester, her parents were politically active. Emmeline Pankhurst's father, Robert Goulden, a calico printer, was a great influence on his daughter. He was interested in the movement for woman suffrage and indeed, her grandfather nearly lost his life in the Peterloo franchise riots in 1819.

In December 1879, she married Richard Pankhurst, a barrister who was 24 years older than her. He was already a supporter of women's right to vote. After having five children in the first ten years of marriage, Emmeline founded and became involved with the Women's Franchise League which advocated suffrage for all women whether married or not. It eventually fell apart and she tried to join the Independent Labour Party through her friendship with the socialist Keir Hardie. However, she was refused membership, on the grounds of her sex, by the local branch of the Party.

By this time Pankhurst was supported by her daughters and along with other Women's Social and Political Union activists they received prison sentences. When incarcerated they often staged hunger strikes.

Pankhurst shared his wife's political views and encouraged her to pursue her reforming activities. They both served on the committee which promoted the Married Women's Property Act. In 1889 Emmeline Pankhurst helped form the Women's Franchise League though this was wound up after a few years.

Initially a Liberal, in 1892 she joined the Independent Labour Party. In 1898 her husband died and she struggled financially in bringing up three daughters and a son. In

1903 her interest in woman suffrage was reawakened by the enthusiasm of her daughter Christabel, so much so that she founded the Women's Social and Political Union.

It pursued a course independent from political parties and became known for its physical confrontations with its members often smashing windows and assaulting police officers.

In 1906, Emmeline and her union began to demonstrate at the House of Commons and were soon involved, not only in clashes with the police, but with the imprisonment of some of their members. For example, in October 1906, she was present at the first of the demonstrations when eleven members of her union were arrested. The violence increased and in January 1908 Emmeline was pelted with and rolled in mud while demonstrating at the Newton Abbot election. She was then arrested while carrying a petition to the Prime Minister at the House of Commons. She was sentenced to six weeks in prison and served five of them. Furthermore, a few months later she was imprisoned again for inciting the public to 'rush' the House of Commons. While serving her three months in Holloway Gaol she led a revolt against the rules of prison discipline.

She received further prison sentences in 1912, first for two months and then for five months. In each case she served only five weeks. However, in 1913 she was arrested on the more serious charge of committing a felony in connection with the blowing-up of Lloyd George's country house at Walton. This time she was sentenced to three years' penal servitude.

She began a hunger strike and then a thirst strike and she was temporarily released. Eventually, after several re-arrests and releases her three year sentence was allowed to lapse in 1914.

Emmeline spent the First World War along with her daughter and many other woman suffrage activists encouraging women to join the nation's fight against Germany.

In November 1913 Emmeline Pankhurst made a speech in Hartford, Connecticut, in which *inter alia* she said:

I do not come here as an advocate, because whatever position the suffrage movement may occupy in the United States of America, in England it has passed beyond the realm of advocacy and it has entered into the sphere of practical politics. It has become the subject of revolution and civil war, and so to-night I am not here to advocate woman suffrage. American suffragists can do that very well for themselves. I am here as a soldier who has temporarily left the field of battle in order to explain – it seems strange it should have to be explained – what civil war is like when civil war is made by women. I am not only here as a soldier temporarily absent from the field of battle; I am here – and that, I think, is the strangest part of my coming – I am here as a person who, according to the law courts of my country, it has been decided, is of no value to the community at all; and I am adjudged because of my life to be a dangerous person, under sentence of penal servitude in a convict prison. So you see there is some special interest in hearing so unusual a person address you. I dare say, in the minds of many of you – you will perhaps forgive me this personal touch – that I do not look either very like a soldier or very like a convict, and yet I am both.

We were determined to press this question of the enfranchisement of the women to the point where we were no longer to be ignored by the politicians as had been the case for about fifty years, during which time women had patiently used every means open to them to win their political enfranchisement.

Time magazine wrote in 1999 that Emmeline Pankhurst was one of the 100 Most Important People of the 20th Century, stating, 'She shaped an idea of women for our time; she shook society into a new pattern from which there could be no going back.'

5. CLEMENT ATTLEE

Clement Attlee was extremely influential largely thanks to his Prime Ministership from 1945 to 1950 when his Labour Government put into practice the nationalisation and social measures advocated by William Beveridge in his report of 1942. This report cited the five giant evils of British society – Want, Disease, Ignorance, Squalor and Idleness.

Beveridge said the cure would come through state-funded social security, a national health service, free education and Government intervention to guarantee full employment and cheap housing. Benefits would be universal, from child benefit to schooling to medical treatment, and the funding would come from a system of national insurance, whereby every employed person paid the same flat rate contribution in return for the same benefits. No other system anywhere in the world rose so high. As Peter, now Lord, Hennessy wrote 'the welfare state became the talisman of a better post-war Britain'.

It was Attlee who made sure all the necessary laws were put in place. What was his background?

He was born in January 1883, the son of Henry Attlee, a solicitor, and was educated at a preparatory school in Kent,

then at the public school Haileybury College and University College, Oxford from where he graduated in 1904 with a Second-Class BA Honours degree in Modern History. He trained as a lawyer and was called to the Bar at Inner Temple in 1906.

How did someone with this upper middle-class upbringing become a socialist?

From 1906 to 1909 he worked as a manager of Haileybury House, a charitable club for working-class boys in Stepney, in London's East End, run by Haileybury College. He was shocked by the poverty he found and came to the conclusion that private charity would never be sufficient to improve the lot of all those deprived citizens. Only the distribution of income enforced by the state would work and consequently Attlee became a supporter of socialism, joining the Independent Labour Party in 1908 and becoming active in local politics.

He served in the Army during the First World War, seeing action both in the Middle East and on the Western Front, and, from 1918 to 1923, lectured at the London School of Economics. At the same time he returned to local politics becoming Mayor of the Metropolitan Borough of Stepney. In the General Election of 1922 he was elected Member of Parliament for Limehouse in Stepney and served as private secretary to Ramsay MacDonald, leader of the Labour Party.

In 1930 when Labour MP Oswald Mosley left the Party to set up his own party, Attlee succeeded him as Chancellor of the Duchy of Lancaster. The Election of 1931 was a disaster for the Labour Party and Attlee, one of the few survivors, became deputy leader under George Lansbury. When Lansbury resigned in 1935, Attlee became interim leader and led the Labour Party through the 1935 Election. In the subsequent leadership election, in spite of the fact that

Herbert Morrison was favourite, Attlee won and was formally declared leader of the Labour Party on 25 October 1935.

When Winston Churchill formed his Coalition Government in 1940 after Neville Chamberlain's resignation following the disastrous Norwegian campaign, Attlee became the Deputy Prime Minister. He was a strong supporter of Churchill throughout the War but, nevertheless, opposed him in the General Election that was called after the defeat of Germany, though before the surrender of Japan.

In the meantime, the Beveridge Report had been published and had sold hundreds of thousands of copies. It secured the official support of both the Conservative and Labour Party but clearly, most voters felt that the Labour Party would be more likely to enact its recommendations and, to the surprise of many, gave Labour power with a very substantial majority in the 1945 General Election.

They were duly rewarded when Attlee did indeed ensure that many of the promised acts of nationalisation were passed. Most significantly, the National Health Service (NHS) was put in place in 1948. This brought a publicly funded healthcare system which offered treatment free of charge for all at the point of use. In its first year the NHS treated no fewer than 8.5 million dental patients and dispensed more than 5 million pairs of spectacles. Working-class people were the major beneficiaries with deaths from diphtheria, pneumonia and TB declining sharply.

Attlee spent his five-year administration passing Acts that put in place Beveridge's plans for a 'cradle to grave' welfare state. The most important, and long-lasting Act, after the NHS, was the National Insurance Act of 1946 in which people in work paid a flat rate of national insurance. In return, they, and their wives, were eligible for flat-rate pensions, sickness benefit, unemployment benefit and funeral benefit.

Other Acts included The New Towns Act of 1946, the Town and Country Planning Act of 1947, The Criminal Act of 1948, The Justice of Peace Act of 1949 and the Legal Aid and Advice Act of 1949.

There was also a great deal of nationalisation in industry and commerce. The Bank of England and civil aviation were nationalised in 1946. In 1947 coal mining, the railways, road haulage, canals and Cable & Wireless were also nationalised and, in 1948, it was the turn of electricity and gas. Finally, the steel industry was nationalised in 1951 by which time about 20 per cent of the British economy had been taken into public ownership.

It all added up to a dramatic change for British society.

4. MARGARET THATCHER

Scarcely a day goes by when Margaret Thatcher is not mentioned on the radio or television or written about in the newspapers. The comments are not always favourable but that does not detract from the influence she had and which she is still having.

Born on 13 October 1925 to Alfred Roberts – and what an influence he had on his daughter – and Beatrice Stephenson (whom Margaret Thatcher failed to mention in her Who's Who entry), she was brought up in the county town of Grantham in Lincolnshire where her father owned two grocery shops. She and her older sister lived with their parents in a flat above one of the shops. Her father was a strong Methodist and also active in local politics. His family were Liberals but Alfred acted in local government as an Independent.

Margaret was educated at Kesteven and Grantham Girls' School, worked hard, was head girl in 1942 and 1943 and tried for a scholarship to study chemistry at Somerville College, Oxford. She was initially rejected but was offered a place when another candidate withdrew. She graduated in 1947 with a Second-Class Honours degree in Chemistry. She was already showing an interest in politics and became President of the Oxford University Conservative Association in 1946. She was also already being influenced by Friedrich von Hayek's book *The Road to Serfdom* in which he condemned economic intervention by government.

Her interest in politics continued and she applied successfully to be adopted as the Conservative candidate for Dartford, Kent in 1950. She lost to the Labour candidate in both the 1950 and 1951 Elections but reduced his majority by 6,000 and then a further 1,000. At this time she met the wealthy businessman Denis Thatcher, and they married in December 1951. He funded Margaret's studies at the Bar and she qualified as a barrister in 1953 specialising in taxation. Also in 1953 she gave birth to twins, Carol and Mark.

Her attempts to become a Conservative MP continued and, eventually, in 1958, she was selected as a candidate for the safe Conservative seat of Finchley in north London. During the 1960s she worked hard and skilfully enough to be appointed Secretary of State for Education by Edward Heath when he won the General Election in 1970.

She started as she meant to continue by imposing cuts on the state education system, for example abolishing free milk for children aged seven to eleven. This earned her the nickname *Margaret Thatcher, Milk Snatcher.* Another nickname she acquired in the 1970s came when she made a speech attacking the Soviet Union. In response the Soviet newspaper *Red Star* referred to her as the *Iron Lady.*

By this time she had succeeded Edward Heath as leader of the Conservative Party when he resigned after the Conservative Party's defeat in the 1974 General Election. Initially she seemed to be having little impact, either against the Labour Prime Minister, Harold Wilson, or against his successor, James Callaghan, who took over in 1976.

Fortunately for her, the general economic conditions deteriorated, the trade union movement seemed to think, with some justification, that they would always win if they went on strike against a Labour Government, and, after what became known as *The Winter of Discontent* in 1978/9, the Conservative Party led by Thatcher won the General Election of May 1979 and she became the country's first female Prime Minister.

At first her Government seemed to be ineffective and Thatcher herself was restrained by the fact that the vast majority of her Cabinet were former Heath supporters and were what she called 'wets'. Furthermore, a further sharp hike in the price of oil by OPEC led to a world recession and unemployment in the UK rose to the unprecedented figure of 3 million.

Her poll rating plummeted and was only rescued by her decision to send troops to win what became known as The Falklands War in the South Atlantic. Far from losing the 1983 Election, which had seemed likely, she won it with an increased majority.

Now, she could implement some of the policies she had longed to introduce. She could also remove from the Cabinet a number of the 'wets' or 'wimps' as she called them. Exchange controls were abolished, many of the nationalised industries were privatised, council homes were sold to their tenants, excessive tax rates for high earners were reduced and the so-called 'big bang' made the City of London more efficient.

There were many problems which she wanted to tackle. Of 25 million people employed in the UK, 7.45 million or 29.3 per cent were in the non-productive public sector, and the Civil Service, employing 738,000, was twice as large as in 1939.

Nationalised industries employed over 2 million, nearly half of the entire number employed in manufacturing industries. Local authorities employed no fewer than 3 million. Britain had the lowest productivity of any major industrial economy with an eight-fold increase in strikes compared with the 1930s.

The term 'Thatcherism' was coined in 1979 and came to mean praise for individual enterprise and suspicion of an interfering state. It meant opposition to any form of collectivism especially if trade unions were involved. There was plenty of opposition even in her own party and in the Cabinet but that did not hold her back. Indeed, she gave the impression she rather enjoyed it and being able to defeat those she viewed as enemies.

One set of people she liked and encouraged, seeing them as vital to the future prosperity of the country, were entrepreneurs and businessmen. One she listened to intently was Sir Alfred Sherman, who had founded the Centre of Policy Studies with her in 1974. Another of her gurus was Sir Keith Joseph who had, like her, been in Edward Heath's Cabinet but, again like her, had opposed his corporation. They pursued the monetarist approach of the Chicago economist Milton Friedman, to control the inflation which had been so damaging to the British economy in the 1970s and early 1980s.

One of Thatcher's great beliefs was the importance of self-help. Ken Clarke, her Minister of Health, said:

She thought it was disgraceful that people who could afford it relied on the taxpayer to provide their healthcare ... she was quite happy that the vulnerable, the poor, should have the taxpayer do it for them. But people like you and me should take responsibility for our own lives and should insure for these things. And anyway it was all part of her great campaign to roll back the frontiers of the state.

Privatisation was a huge and successful project in the Thatcher era. To her it was key in reducing the power of the trade unions and it formed a key part of her plan to show unions and indeed management that industry was going to have to improve if it was to cope with the increasing competition from companies overseas.

Between 1979 and 1990 no less than 60 per cent of the state sector of industry was privatised. Thatcher herself wrote in her autobiography, 'It constituted the greatest shift of ownership and power away from the state to individuals and their families in any country outside the former communist bloc. Indeed Britain set a worldwide trend in privatisation in countries as different as Czechoslovakia and New Zealand.'

Margaret Thatcher foresaw that the problem with socialism is that you eventually run out of other people's money.

Thatcher's influence also spread overseas where countries, including, ironically, a number of countries in the former Eastern Europe, as well as others in Mexico, Brazil and the Far East, adopted Thatcherite policies and especially privatisation.

In conclusion, Britain went into the Thatcher era a dispirited, overmanned, union-bullied, under-managed, poorly performing, bureaucratised, inefficient, subsidised, benefit-demanding, class-ridden society, living with the comforting certainties of the Cold War, and came out of it a lively, relatively lean, union-cowed, well-managed, reasonably performing, not-quite-so bureaucratised, less inefficient, though still hopelessly subsidised and benefit-demanding class-ridden society, facing the uncertain realities of freed Communist states, most of which quickly adopted Thatcherite practice.

3. WILLIAM BEVERIDGE

William Beveridge was born on 5 March 1879 in Bengal, India, where his father was a judge in the Indian Civil Service. He was educated at Charterhouse and Balliol College, Oxford and later trained as a lawyer.

His interest in the causes of unemployment began in 1903 and, working closely with Sidney and Beatrice Webb, he was influenced by their theories of social reform. He campaigned for old age pensions, free school meals and a national system of labour exchanges and first came to prominence during the Liberal Government of 1906–14 when he was asked to advise David Lloyd George on old age pensions and national insurance. During the First World War, Beveridge was involved in mobilising and controlling manpower. In 1919, he became a director of the London School of Economics and remained there until 1937.

He retained his contacts with Fabian Society socialists and, in 1939, published a historical study of prices and wages.

In the Second World War, the Minister of Labour in the National Government, Ernest Bevin, invited Beveridge to take charge of the Welfare department of his Ministry. Although Bevin and Beveridge did not get on together very well, Beveridge became Chairman of a committee of officials to survey existing social insurance and allied services.

In 1942 Beveridge's report to Parliament on Social Insurance and Allied Services was published. It proposed that all people of working age should pay a weekly national insurance contribution. In return, benefits would be paid to people who were sick, unemployed, retired or widowed. Beveridge maintained that this system would provide a minimum standard of living 'below which no one should be allowed to fall'. It also recommended that the Government should find ways of fighting what he called the five 'Giant Evils' – Want, Disease, Ignorance, Squalor and Idleness. He also recommended the formation of a National Health Service.

These recommendations were obviously attractive to the less well-off and underprivileged and Beveridge worked hard to persuade the better-off and the sceptics by saying that welfare institutions would increase the competitiveness of British industry after the War, not only by moving healthcare and pension costs on to the state but also by producing healthier, more prosperous and therefore more motivated and productive workers. This increased prosperity would increase demand for British goods.

Not everyone was convinced. Leading industrialists argued that the aim of fighting Germany was to stop them installing the Gestapo in Britain not to build an expensive welfare state. Furthermore, the Conservative Chancellor of the Exchequer, Sir Kingsley Wood, told Prime Minister Winston Churchill that the country could not afford Beveridge's plan.

Nevertheless, when Beveridge's long, detailed report was published, it sold like no other Government report before or since: 100,000 copies were sold within a month and eventually

over 600,000 copies were bought. A Gallup survey in 1943 showed that 19 out of 20 people knew about the Beveridge Plan. It was distributed to British troops and dropped over occupied Europe by Lancaster bombers. Incredibly, a detailed analysis of the Beveridge Report was found in Hitler's bunker at the end of the War, which described it as 'superior to the current German social insurance in almost all points'.

In 1945 when the Labour Party won the General Election, the new Prime Minister, Clement Attlee, began the process of implementing the Beveridge Report and the modern welfare state was born (interestingly, Beveridge himself never referred to the 'Welfare' state, but rather he used the term 'social service state'). The benefits were universal, covering child benefit, schooling and medical treatment. The funding came from a system of national insurance by which every employed person paid the flat-rate contribution in return for the same benefits. The well-known historian Peter Hennessy described it as 'the talisman of a better post-war Britain'. By the end of the 1950s the National Health Service (NHS) was regarded as a national treasure and has remained so ever since. It bore out the principle 'to each according to his needs, from each according to his abilities'.

2. JOHN MAYNARD KEYNES

John Maynard Keynes was the most influential economist of the 20th century. His economic theories sprang from his direct practical experience of the three key moments in that century: the post-Second World War peace settlement, the Great Depression of the 1930s and the Second World War.

Keynes was born in June 1883 at 6 Harvey Road, Cambridge, a house built by his parents and his mother lived there until she died in 1958, twelve years after her son Maynard died. Keynes's father, John Neville Keynes, was an assistant to the economists Alfred Marshall and Henry Sidgwick.

Keynes showed early intellectual promise correcting his aunt's English when he was only five. After prep school at the Perse and St Faith's in Cambridge he went to Eton as a scholar, mainly on the strength of his maths. At Eton he won many prizes including all the school's main maths prizes. He also acquired an excellent command of English.

In 1902 Keynes gained an Open Scholarship to King's College, Cambridge where he was invited to join the University's most exclusive society, *The Cambridge Conversazione Society* or *Apostles*, whose object was the pursuit of truth with absolute devotion. After Cambridge he joined the Civil Service and became a junior clerk in the military department of the India Office in 1906.

After finding little satisfaction in this job, he returned to Cambridge in 1909 thanks to a prize fellowship at King's on the basis of his theories on probability. In 1911 he became editor of the *Economic Journal* and, in 1912, was elected a member of the select Political Economy Club.

Up to the outbreak of war in 1914 Keynes did not attempt to develop monetary theory beyond the stage reached by Alfred Marshall, the founder of English academic economies. Marshall said that the very rich and the very poor were the ignoble elements of society and that both should be eliminated through the redistribution of wealth.

On the outbreak of war in August 1914, Keynes moved to the Treasury and was soon giving advice at the highest level. Indeed, it could be argued that he was instrumental in bringing the Americans into the War, by persuading the British Government

to maintain convertibility in early 1917. The Americans liked that since they had most of the world's gold.

After four years of horrendous slaughter the Germans capitulated at the eleventh hour of the eleventh day in the eleventh month of 1918 and their future would be determined at the Paris Peace Conference in Versailles in 1919. The leaders of the victorious countries, Woodrow Wilson of the USA, Georges Clémenceau of France and David Lloyd George of Great Britain, recommended that Germany should pay 'the full cost of its aggression', and a figure of £24 billion (£1,000 billion today) was demanded.

Keynes thought this was appalling and declared 'That's ridiculous! Damn nincompoop bankers!' His team produced numbers which showed Germany's capacity to pay was about £3 billion and suggested that the Allies would be lucky to get £2 billion. Keynes said, 'If Germany is to be milked she must not, first of all, be ruined.'

He resigned from the Treasury and wrote *The Economic Consequences of the Peace*, one of the most important and influential books of the 20th century.

This book which demonstrated that Germany could only afford to pay £2 billion over three years became world famous. Many, such as Arthur Pigou, who succeeded Marshall as Professor of Political Economy at Cambridge, were full of praise. Pigou himself said, 'Absolutely splendid and quite unanswerable!' However, others said its influence damaged world affairs, saying 'It weakened British and French resistance to Hitler, because it agrees with him that the Versailles Treaty was unfair.' 'It gave America an argument for abandoning Europe to its fate', while Hitler felt, 'It gave me an excuse to break the Treaty.'

The next test for Keynes was Britain's return to the Gold Standard at the pound sterling's pre-War dollar parity of

$4.86. The Federation of British Industry (FBI) were in favour: 'A return to the Gold Standard would be greatly to our benefit.' Bankers agreed: 'The Gold Standard will restore the City and Sterling to their former pre-eminence.' This was echoed by the Treasury: 'Only a world recovery will bring a reduction in unemployment ... but a world recovery depends on stable exchange rates.'

Keynes was against it and was proved right. Later, almost everyone agreed that the £ was overvalued between 1925 and 1931 leading to a fall in exports and a rise in unemployment.

Finally, the world depression of the 1930s led to Keynes writing *The General Theory of Unemployment, Interest, and Money*, published in 1936. If his *Economic Consequences of the Peace* was *one* of the most influential books of the 20th century, *The General Theory* is *the* most influential.

To Keynes it was more sensible to employ people to do something – anything – as long as they were paid, rather than have them stand idle and be paid little or nothing. He also propounded the Multiplier. This is the individual's propensity to consume which is the fraction of an individual's *increase* spent on consumption.

Ironically, the country that put Keynesian economics into practice to the greatest effect in the 1930s was Hitler's Germany. In 1932 industrial output in Germany was 40 per cent below 1929 and there were 6 million people unemployed. By 1938 output was 25 per cent above the 1929 level and unemployment had been virtually eliminated.

After the tragedy of the Second World War, the British Government pursued what it perceived to be Keynesian policies. Through the 1940s, 1950s and 1960s every Government, Labour or Conservative, held full employment as its most important priority and, indeed, to most, still to this day, it remains the most important.

1. SIR TIM BERNERS-LEE

Every owner of a computer throughout the world has been influenced by Sir Tim Berners-Lee, the inventor of the World Wide Web or www.

The internet today is a combination of technologies but Berners-Lee's vision was a worldwide hypertext or the computer aided reading of electronic documents which would allow people to work together even though they lived thousands of miles apart. They would share their knowledge in a web of documents. His achievement was to give the internet's hardware a global voice.

Timothy Berners-Lee was born in London on 8 June 1955. His parents were Mary and Conway who had met in Manchester in 1953 when they were both working on the Ferranti Mark 1 computer. This was the first computer in the world to go on sale. Nine machines were bought by large corporations. Mary was a programmer so she gave Mark 1 its instructions.

The Ferranti Mark 1 was no less than 5 metres, or 17 feet, long and 2.7 metres, or nine feet, high. It was so heavy that floors beneath it usually had to be reinforced.

Timothy soon had two brothers, Peter and Michael, and a sister, Helen. The family lived in East Sheen, a suburb of London. As soon as the children could talk their parents involved them in mathematics and turned everything into a mathematical game. Tim recalled, 'The whole point about mathematics in our house was that it was fun.' And he remembered that when he visited his father's office he fell in love with his giant computer and, at home, built his own pretend computer from cardboard boxes and rolls of old computer tape.

At only four Tim started at his local primary school and made friends with Nicholas Barton. They were both fascinated by science and encouraged each other to read encyclopaedias and report their findings. They soon discovered a book by Leonard de Vries called *The Book of Experiments* which was full of experiments that could be done at home and Tim, Nick and a friend called Christopher carried them out learning about things such as air pressure and forces.

In 1966 Tim won a place at Emanuel School in Wandsworth Common. He was slightly worried at first because it meant he had to travel there by train every day while all his friends were at a local school. However, he soon became fascinated by trains. Seeing this, his parents bought him an electric train set and Tim was soon taking the trains apart to study the electronics. Wanting his trains to whistle he learned how to wire two transistors back to back so that they made a whistling sound.

While at Emanuel Tim did not enjoy rugby and cricket but he did play for the school. At eighteen he went up to Queen's College, Oxford to study physics. Ironically, although he worked hard, he got into trouble over a computer. It was caused by his helping organise Rag Week with Pete, a friend. At the time the University had just one computer room, with one printer which was only supposed to be used for important work. Tim and Pete sneaked into the room to print a heap of information for Rag Week. As they were doing so the computer crashed. The boys were caught and were banned from ever using the computers again.

In spite of this, Tim was determined to have use of a computer and, as they were expensive, decided to build his own. For the keyboard he adapted a calculator keypad and for the monitor he paid £5 (£100 today). Microprocessors,

which act as a brain of a computer, storing instructions and processing information, had recently gone on sale and Tim saved up to buy one using his wages from a holiday job in a sawmill. By the time he graduated with a First-Class Honours degree he had built his own computer.

It was now 1976 and as Tim looked for his first job at the electronics company Plessey, he noted that the use of microprocessors meant that computers no longer had to be huge and expensive. The first personal computers, known as PCs, were going on sale. Tim gradually became an expert in programming computer software, that is, all the programs that operate a computer and make it useful.

Tim became restless and he and his wife, Jane, divorced. They had met at Oxford and had married when both joined Plessey. Looking for a new job he joined the European Organization for Nuclear Research, CERN, in Switzerland in 1980. CERN was a giant physics laboratory where scientists from all over the world carried out experiments into the nature of atoms and the tiny particles inside them.

He did not have his own computer on his desk so, whenever he needed to program, he had to go to the computer in the central control room. Some employees brought their own computers but at that time there was no way in which these computers could be linked to form a network within the organisation. It was not until the end of the 1980s that CERN was finally able to take advantage of the early version of what we now know as the internet, although in those days it was limited to the sending of simple messages between the world's 1 million internet users. In spite of this progress, there was still no efficient way in which the 5,000 scientists at CERN could share more sophisticated information among themselves or the outside world.

It was Tim Berners-Lee who put forward a solution in

March 1989. He suggested he create a system which would allow general communication using hypertext to create links between different pages of information. Hypertext was not new but Berners-Lee was the first to propose marrying the internet with hypertext. He realised that his system could change the way people shared ideas and not just at CERN but throughout the world.

In looking for a name, he suggested World Wide Web and this was accepted by his boss at CERN. Tim then created a language for writing hypertext and called it Hypertext Markup Language or HTML. To allow people to view websites on their own computers, he needed to make rules for sending hypertext documents over the internet. He called these rules Hypertext Transport Protocol or HTTP. Furthermore he needed a system of addresses to identify websites. Each website would therefore be given a Uniform Resource Locator, or URL.

To measure the growth of the World Wide Web – in 1993 there were about 620 websites; five years later Google had indexed 26 million pages and ten years after that a million million, or 1 trillion; in 1989 there were around a million internet users; by 2015 there were over 3 billion.

Berners-Lee made that possible. He did toy with the idea of starting a company to make money out of the growing Web and he started to discuss setting up a group to oversee the Web, sponsored by the Massachusetts Institute of Technology (MIT) in the USA. In 1994, he moved with his family (he had remarried in 1990 to Nancy Carlson and by 1994 they had two children, Alice and Ben) to Massachusetts so that he could lead the World Wide Web Consortium or W3C.

John Naughton summed up the man himself in the *Observer*:

This is a man who invented the future, who created something which one day will be bigger than all the other industries on earth. This is a man whose intellectual property rights could have made him richer than Bill Gates and Warren Buffett combined. And yet he turned his back on all that in order to work for the common good.

Tim Berners-Lee's innovation of the World Wide Web is unique. It has given the world an immense Information Marketplace. Newspapers, radio and television can hardly compare. Nor can letters or the telephone. Gutenberg's printing, Bell's telephone and Marconi's radio were great achievements but what Berners-Lee has achieved surpasses them all and is unique.